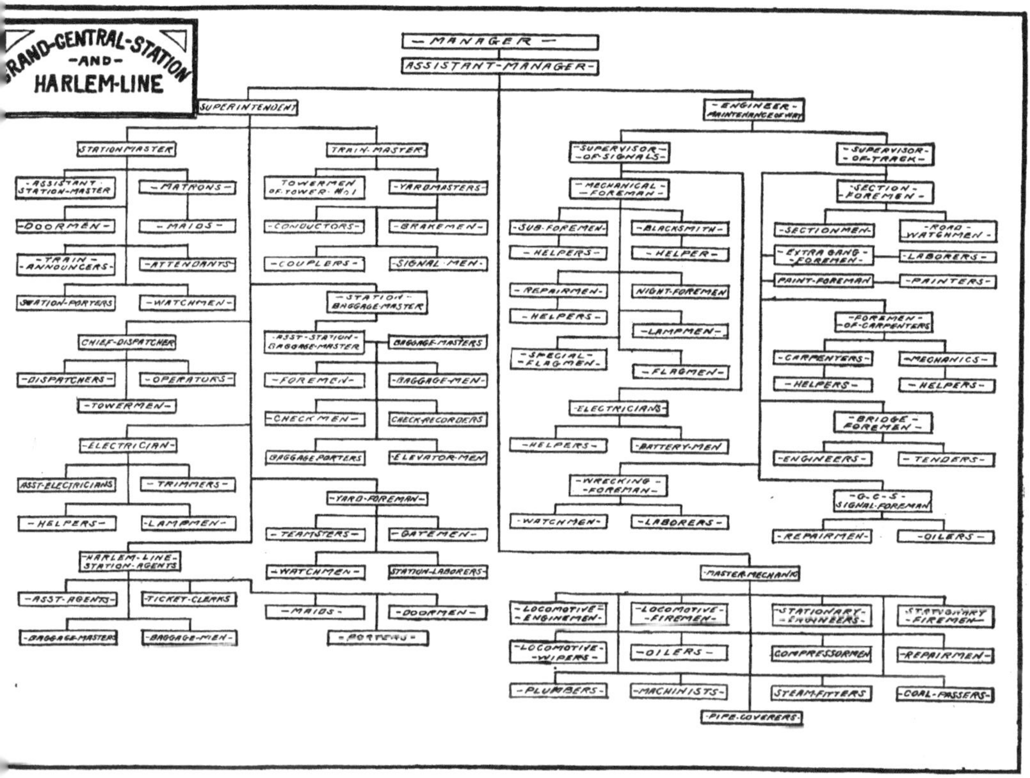

GRAND-CENTRAL-STATION -AND- HARLEM-LINE

- MANAGER
  - ASSISTANT-MANAGER
    - SUPERINTENDENT
      - STATIONMASTER
        - ASSISTANT STATION-MASTER
        - MATRONS
        - DOORMEN
        - MAIDS
        - TRAIN-ANNOUNCERS
        - ATTENDANTS
        - STATION-PORTERS
        - WATCHMEN
      - CHIEF-DISPATCHER
        - DISPATCHERS
        - OPERATORS
        - TOWERMEN
      - ELECTRICIAN
        - ASST-ELECTRICIANS
        - TRIMMERS
        - HELPERS
        - LAMPMEN
      - HARLEM-LINE-STATION-AGENTS
        - ASST-AGENTS
        - TICKET-CLERKS
        - BAGGAGE-MASTERS
        - BAGGAGE-MEN
      - TRAIN-MASTER
        - TOWERMEN OF TOWER No 1
        - YARDMASTERS
        - CONDUCTORS
        - BRAKEMEN
        - COUPLERS
        - SIGNAL MEN
      - STATION BAGGAGE-MASTER
        - ASST-STATION-BAGGAGE-MASTER
        - BAGGAGE-MASTERS
        - FOREMEN
        - BAGGAGE-MEN
        - CHECK MEN
        - CHECK-RECORDERS
        - BAGGAGE PORTERS
        - ELEVATOR-MEN
      - YARD-FOREMAN
        - TEAMSTERS
        - GATEMEN
        - WATCHMEN
        - STATION-LABORERS
      - MAIDS
      - DOORMEN
      - PORTERS
    - ENGINEER MAINTENANCE OF WAY
      - SUPERVISOR OF SIGNALS
        - MECHANICAL FOREMAN
          - SUB-FOREMEN
          - BLACKSMITH
          - HELPERS
          - HELPER
          - REPAIRMEN
          - NIGHT-FOREMEN
          - HELPERS
          - LAMPMEN
          - SPECIAL FLAGMEN
          - FLAGMEN
        - ELECTRICIANS
          - HELPERS
          - BATTERY-MEN
        - WRECKING FOREMAN
          - WATCHMEN
          - LABORERS
      - SUPERVISOR OF TRACK
        - SECTION FOREMEN
          - SECTIONMEN
          - ROAD WATCHMEN
          - EXTRA GANG FOREMEN
          - LABORERS
          - PAINT-FOREMAN
          - PAINTERS
        - FOREMEN OF CARPENTERS
          - CARPENTERS
          - MECHANICS
          - HELPERS
          - HELPERS
        - BRIDGE FOREMEN
          - ENGINEERS
          - TENDERS
        - G-C-S SIGNAL-FOREMAN
          - REPAIRMEN
          - OILERS
    - MASTER MECHANIC
      - LOCOMOTIVE ENGINEMEN
      - LOCOMOTIVE FIREMEN
      - STATIONARY ENGINEERS
      - STATIONARY FIREMEN
      - LOCOMOTIVE WIPERS
      - OILERS
      - COMPRESSORMEN
      - REPAIRMEN
      - PLUMBERS
      - MACHINISTS
      - STEAM-FITTERS
      - COAL-PASSERS
      - PIPE-COVERERS

RULES OF THE

GRAND CENTRAL STATION

AND

HARLEM LINE

FOR THE GOVERNMENT

OF THE

EMPLOYES

SUPERSEDING ALL
EXISTING ORDERS OR INSTRUCTIONS
INCONSISTENT THEREWITH

TO TAKE EFFECT
JANUARY 1, 1904

THE DE VINNE PRESS
IMPRIMATVR

INDEX.

THE rules herein set forth govern all employes of the Grand Central Station and Harlem Line, and employes of the New York Central & Hudson River Railroad, and the New York, New Haven & Hartford Railroad Companies, while at the Grand Central Station or on the Harlem Line.

IRA A. McCORMACK,
Manager.

GENERAL NOTICE.

TO enter, or remain in, the service is an assurance of willingness to obey the rules.

Obedience to the rules is essential to the safety of Passengers and Employes, and to the protection of property.

The service demands the faithful, intelligent and courteous discharge of duty.

To obtain promotion capacity must be shown for greater responsibility.

Employes are advised that, in accepting employment, they assume the accompanying risks, and are expected to look after, and be responsible for, their own safety, as well as to exercise the utmost caution to avoid injury to others.

The safety of Passengers and Trains is of the first importance, and all operations of working, repairing, or constructing this road must be subservient thereto. To this, with the regularity and punctuality of the Trains, and the comfort and convenience of Patrons, all work must be entirely subordinate.

It is of the utmost importance that proper rules for the government of the employes of a railroad company should be enforced, in order to make such rules efficient. If they cannot or ought not to be enforced, they ought not to exist. Officers or employes whose duty it may be to make or enforce rules, however temporary or unimportant they may seem, should keep this clearly in mind. If in the judgment of any one whose duty it is to enforce a rule, such rule cannot or ought not to be enforced, he should at once bring it to the attention of those in authority.

Special instructions may be issued by proper authority.

All employes are required to be polite and considerate in their intercourse with the public. The reputation and prosperity of the Company depend greatly upon the promptness with which its business is conducted, and the manner in which the public is treated by its employes.

GENERAL RULES.

GENERAL RULES.

A Employes whose duties are prescribed by these rules must provide themselves with a copy.

B Employes must be conversant with and obey the rules and special instructions. If in doubt as to their meaning, they must apply to proper authority for an explanation.

C Employes must pass the required examinations.

D Persons employed in any service on trains are subject to the rules and special instructions.

E Employes must render every assistance in their power in carrying out the rules and special instructions.

F Any violation of the rules or special instructions must be reported.

G The use of intoxicants by employes while on duty is prohibited. Their habitual use, or the frequenting of places where they are sold, is sufficient cause for dismissal.

H The use of tobacco by employes when on duty in or about passenger stations or on passenger cars is prohibited.

J Employes when on duty must wear the prescribed badge and uniform and be neat in appearance.

K Persons authorized to transact business at stations or on trains must be orderly and avoid annoyance to passengers.

L In case of danger to the Company's property, employes must unite to protect it.

M All persons whose duties are in any way affected by the time-tables, must have a copy of the current time-table with them when on duty.

N When a person is discharged from the company's service he will not be re-employed without the consent of the officer who dismissed him, or that of the head of the department from which he was discharged.

O If an employe should be disabled by sickness or other cause, the right to claim compensation will not be recognized. An allowance, if made, will be a gratuity justified by the circumstances of the case and the employe's previous good conduct.

P No employe is allowed to contract any bill or other obligation on account of the Company, or to use the Company's credit, unless authorized by the proper officer.

Q Employes are required to inform themselves respecting the location of all structures or obstructions along the line that will not clear them when on the top or sides of cars or engines; also as to the conditions of equipment and track.

They are also required to know that all brake wheels, dogs, grab irons, hand holds, steps, and other appliances used in the line of their duty are secure and in safe condition before using same.

Employes are warned that extra and special trains may run at any time, and trains may run on any track in either direction without notice, except to those whom it is necessary to advise in order to insure proper movement of such trains. Employes must be governed accordingly, and exercise proper care to avoid being injured.

R Every employe, while on duty connected with the trains on any division of the road, is under the authority and must conform to the orders of the superintendent of that division.

S Employes are required to keep the premises in their charge in a neat and orderly condition.

T No employe will be allowed to absent himself from duty without special permission from the head of the department in which he is employed, nor will any employe be allowed to engage a substitute to perform his duties.

U In the selection of new men for the service, as in the case of station men, signalmen, brakemen, firemen, or of apprentices, care should be taken to get only persons of good character, and who give promise of being able to improve and to deserve promotion. No person should be employed in such service who cannot write and read writing with ease. Applications for employment should be made on the prescribed form.

V Minors must not be employed in any department except in the shops, stations, and offices, and then only after the written consent of their parents or guardians has been obtained.

W The assignment or attaching of an employe's wages by garnishee process or proceedings in aid of execution will be considered sufficient cause for dismissal, unless a satisfactory explanation is given.

X All articles furnished by the Company for use of employes must, on leaving the service, be returned to the proper officer. The right is reserved to withhold from wages due the value of such articles lost or that are not surrendered on leaving the service.

Y Rules issued to individual classes must be observed by all employes should they relate in any way to the proper discharge of their duties.

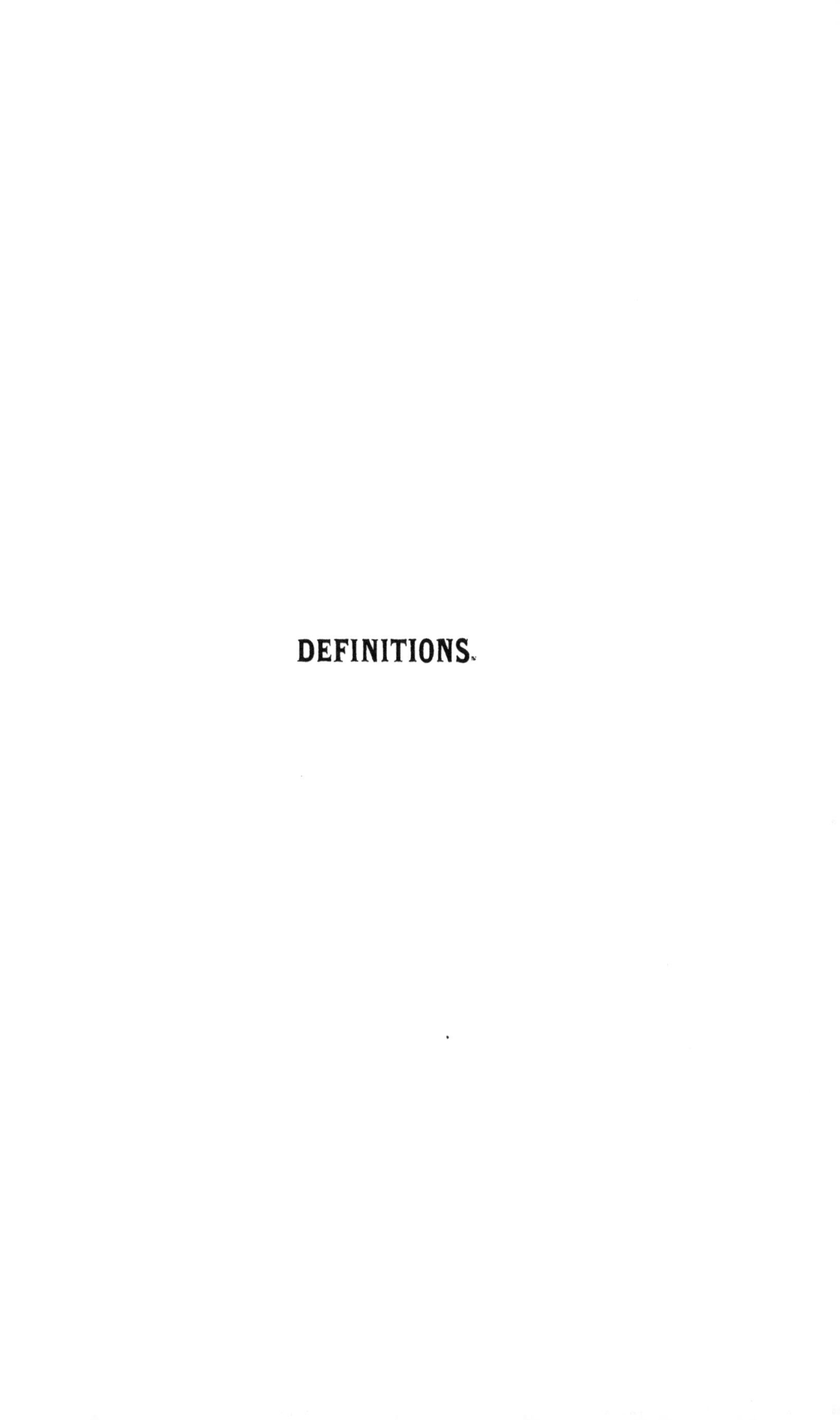

DEFINITIONS.

DEFINITIONS.

TRAIN.—An engine, or more than one engine coupled, with or without cars, displaying Markers.

REGULAR TRAIN.—A train represented on the Time-table. It may consist of sections.

SECTION.—One of two or more trains running on the same schedule displaying signals or for which signals are displayed.

EXTRA TRAIN.—A train not represented on the Time-table. It may be designated as—

Extra—for any extra train, except work extra.

Work extra—for work train extra.

SUPERIOR TRAIN.—A train having precedence over other trains.

NOTE.—Superiority by direction is limited to single track.

A train may be made superior to another train by RIGHT, CLASS or DIRECTION.

RIGHT is conferred by train order; CLASS and DIRECTION by time-table.

RIGHT is superior to CLASS or DIRECTION. DIRECTION is superior as between trains of the same class.

TRAIN OF SUPERIOR RIGHT.—A train given precedence by train order.

TRAIN OF SUPERIOR CLASS.—A train given precedence by time-table.

2

Train of Superior Direction.—A train given precedence in the direction specified in the Time-table as between trains of the same class.

Note.—Superiority by direction is limited to single track.

Time-table.—The authority for the movement of regular trains subject to the rules. It contains the classified schedules of trains with special instructions relating thereto.

Markers.—A green flag or a green light to the front and side, and two or more red lights to the rear.

Schedule.—That part of a Time-table which prescribes the class, direction, number and movement of a regular train.

Main Track.—A principal track upon which trains are operated by time-table, train orders, or by block signals.

Single Track.—A main track upon which trains are operated in both directions.

Double Track.—Two main tracks, upon one of which the current of traffic is in a specified direction, and upon the other in the opposite direction.

Current of Traffic.—The direction in which trains will move on a main track, under the rules.

Station.—A place designated on the time-table by name, at which a train may stop for traffic; or to enter or leave the main track; or from which fixed signals are operated.

Yard.—A system of tracks within defined limits provided for the making up of trains, storing of cars and other purposes, over which movements not authorized by time-table, or by train order, may be made, subject to prescribed signals and regulations.

YARD ENGINE.—An engine assigned to yard service and working within yard limits.

PILOT.—A person assigned to a train when the engineman or conductor, or both, are not fully acquainted with the physical characteristics, or running rules of the road, or portion of the road, over which the train is to be moved.

FIXED SIGNAL.—A signal of fixed location, indicating a condition affecting the movement of a train.

INTERLOCKING.—An arrangement of switch, lock and signal appliances so interconnected that their movements must succeed each other in a predetermined order.

INTERLOCKING PLANT.—An assemblage of switch, lock and signal appliances interlocked.

INTERLOCKING STATION.—A place from which an interlocking plant is operated.

INTERLOCKING SIGNALS.—The fixed signals of an interlocking plant.

BLOCK.—A length of track of defined limits, the use of which by trains is controlled by block signals.

BLOCK STATION.—A place from which block signals are operated.

BLOCK SIGNAL.—A fixed signal controlling the use of a block.

BLOCK SYSTEM.—A series of consecutive blocks.

TELEGRAPH BLOCK SYSTEM.—A block system in

which the signals are operated manually, upon information by telegraph.

Controlled Manual Block System.—A block system in which the block signals are operated manually, and so constructed as to require the co-operation of the signalmen at both ends of the block to display a clear signal.

Automatic Block System.—A block system in which the signals are operated by electric, pneumatic or other agency actuated by a train, or by certain conditions affecting the use of a block.

Home Signal.—A fixed signal controlling the entrance to a block or governing movements over switches at interlockings.

Distant Signal.—A fixed signal used in connection with home and advance signals to regulate the approach thereto.

Advance Signal.—A fixed signal placed in advance of the home signal or switches at an interlocking to control the entrance to the block ahead.

Dwarf Signal.—A low fixed signal.

Pot Signal.—A revolving signal.

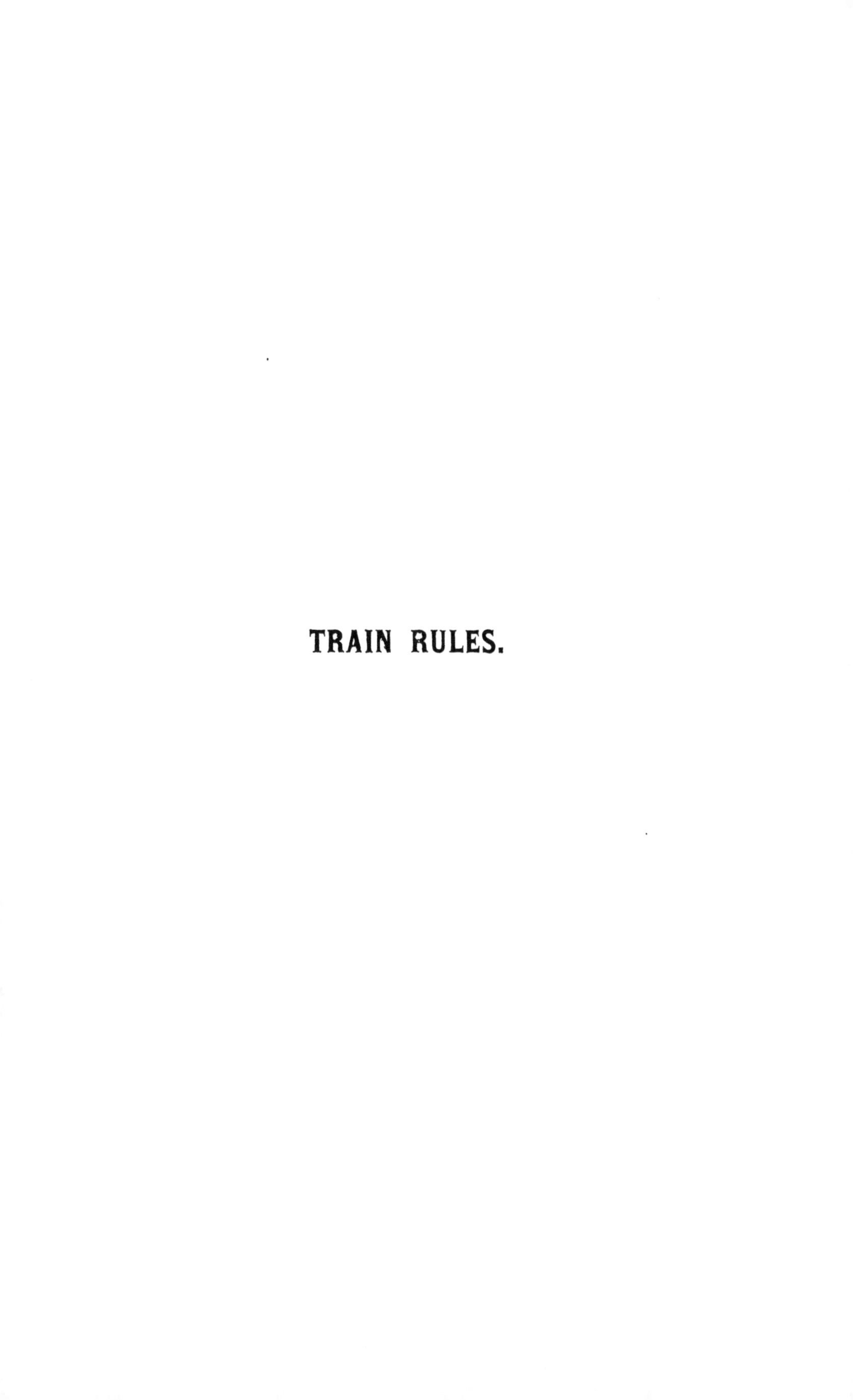

TRAIN RULES.

STANDARD TIME.

1 Standard Time obtained from the Washington, D. C., observatory will be telegraphed to all points from designated offices at 12 noon daily. Standard time.

2 Watches that have been examined and certified to by a designated inspector must be used by conductors, enginemen, yard-masters, station-masters, supervisors, section foremen, and such others who may be designated. The certificate in prescribed form must be renewed and filed with Superintendent every six months (January and July). Examination of watches. Renewal of certificate.

[FORM OF CERTIFICATE.]

Certificate of Watch Inspector.

This is to certify that on .... 19.... the watch of ....
employed as .... was examined by me. It is correct and reliable and, in my judgment, will, with proper care, run within a variation of thirty seconds per week. Form of certificate.

Name of maker ....
Brand ....
Number of movement ....
Open or hunting case ....
Metal of case ....
Stem or key winding ....
(Signed)

....
Inspector.

Address ....

Bi-weekly inspection.

3 Each employe whose watch is subject to inspection must report to an inspector every two weeks, and oftener when convenient, in order that the condition of his watch may be noted and a record of its performance made on proper form and company's record book by inspector.

Comparison with Standard Clock.

4 Watches of conductors and enginemen must be compared, before starting on each trip, with a clock designated as a Standard Clock. The time when watches are compared must be registered on a prescribed form, and any variation must be shown.

Obtaining standard time.

5 Conductors and enginemen whose duties prevent them from having access to a standard clock must compare daily with, and take the time from, the watches of conductors and enginemen who have standard time and have registered their names as provided above. Conductors and enginemen of trains which have been laid up eight or more hours, and who have not had an opportunity to compare their watches as provided, must receive standard time from one of the designated offices before commencing their runs.

Time-tables.

Superseding

6 Each Time-table, from the moment it takes effect, supersedes the preceding Time-table. A train of the preceding Time-table shall retain its train orders and take the schedule of the train of the same number on the new Time-table.

Train of new time-table.

A train of the new Time-table which has not the same number on the preceding Time-table shall not run on any division (or district) until it is due to start from its initial station on that division (or district) after the Time-table takes effect.

Signal Rules.

7 All employes of the railroads terminating at the Grand Central Station or running over the Harlem Line must make themselves familiar with the location and meaning of all signals, and the rules governing the same, before attempting to discharge any duties requiring such information. Familiarize.

8 Conductors will be held strictly responsible for the safety of their trains, and in case of stoppage upon any part of the line they must positively know that their trains are protected. Safety of train.

9 Employes whose duties may require them to give signals, must provide themselves with the proper appliances, and keep them in good order and always ready for immediate use. Employes have proper appliances.

10 Flags of the prescribed color must be used by day, and lamps of the prescribed color by night. Flags and lamps.

11 Night signals are to be displayed from sunset to sunrise. When weather or other conditions obscure day signals, night signals must be used in addition. Night signals

12 Night signals must be used in the Tunnel at all times.

VISIBLE SIGNALS.

13 Color Signals.

Color signals

COLOR.	INDICATION.
(*a*) Red.	Stop.
(*b*) White.	Proceed, and for other uses prescribed by the Rules.
(*c*) Green.	Proceed with caution, and for other uses prescribed by the Rules.
(*d*) Blue.	See Rule 31.

14 Hand, Flag and Lamp Signals.

Hand signals

Manner of Using.		Indication.
(*a*) Swung across the track.	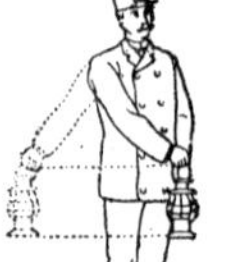	Stop.
(*b*) Raised and lowered vertically.		Proceed.

(*c*) Swung vertically in a circle across the track, when the train is standing.

Back.

(*d*) Swung vertically in a circle at arm's length across the track, when the train is running.

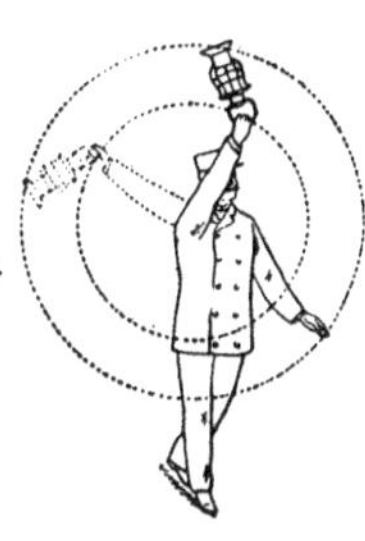

Train has parted.

(*e*) Swung horizontally in a circle, when the train is standing.

Apply air brakes.

(*f*) Held at arm's length above the head, when train is standing.

Release air brakes.

Stop signal. **15** Any object waved violently by any one on or near the track is a signal to stop.

AUDIBLE SIGNALS.

Engine whistle signals.

16 Engine Steam Whistle Signals.

NOTE.—The signals prescribed are illustrated by "o" for short sounds; "——" for longer sounds. The sound of the whistle should be distinct, with intensity and duration proportionate to the distance signal is to be conveyed.

SOUND.	INDICATION.
(*a*) o	Stop. Apply brakes.
(*b*) — —	Release brakes.
(*c*) —— o o o	Flagman go back and protect rear of train.
(*d*) — — — —	Flagman return from south.
(*e*) — — — — —	Flagman return from north.
(*f*) — — —	When running, train parted; to be repeated until answered by the signal prescribed by rule 14 (*d*). Answer to 14 (*d*).
(*g*) o o	Answer to any signal not otherwise provided for.
(*h*) o o o	When train is standing, back. Answer to 14 (*c*) and 20 (*c*).
(*j*) o o o o	Call for signals.

Alarm signal. **17** A succession of short sounds of the whistle is an alarm for persons or cattle on the track, and calls the attention of trainmen to danger ahead.

Torpedoes. **18** The explosion of one or more torpedoes is a signal to **stop** immediately; if between block signals, and track is found to be clear, proceed with caution to the next fixed signal; if at a home signal, proceed only when signal is cleared, or when clearance card has been received by the Engineman.

19 Torpedoes must not be placed near stations or road crossings where persons are liable to be injured by them.

20 Air-whistle or Bell-cord Signals.

Air-whistle signals.

SOUND.	INDICATION.
(*a*) Two.	When train is standing, start.
(*b*) Two.	When train is running, stop at once.
(*c*) Three.	When train is standing, back the train.
(*d*) Three.	When train is running, stop at next station. To be answered as per 16 (*g*).
(*e*) Four.	When train is standing, apply or release air brakes.
(*f*) Four.	When train is running, reduce speed.
(*g*) Five.	When train is standing, call in flagman.
(*h*) Five.	When train is running, increase speed.
(*j*) Six.	When train is running, increase steam heat.

Train Signals.

21 The headlight will be displayed to the front of every train. Displaying headlight.

22 Yard engines will display the headlight to the front and rear by night, or when weather conditions Signals carried on yard engines render it necessary. When not provided with a headlight at the rear, two white lights must be displayed. Yard engines will not display markers.

Markers.

23 The following signals will be displayed, one on each side of the rear of every train, as markers, to indicate the rear of the train: a green flag or a green light to the front and side and a red light to the rear.

Special Harlem Line markers.

24 In addition to regular Markers as prescribed by Rule 23, the following special rules must have strict observance:

24-a When an engine is running backward without cars a white light must be displayed on the rear of the tender and two red lights on the front of the engine. The headlight must be extintinguished or concealed.

24-b When an engine is running forward without cars the headlight must be displayed, and two red lights must be displayed on the rear of the tender.

24-c If an engine running backward is coupled to the rear of a shop train, two red lights must be displayed on the front of the engine, and headlight extinguished or concealed.

24-d If an engine running forward is coupled to the rear of a shop train, two red lights must be displayed on the rear of the tender.

Sections displaying signals.

25 All sections of a train, except the last, will display two green flags and, in addition, two green lights by night in the places provided for that purpose on the front of the engine.

26 Extra trains will display two white flags and, in addition, two white lights by night in the places provided for that purpose on the front of the engine. Extra train signals.

27 When two or more engines are coupled to the head of a train, each engine shall display the signals as prescribed by the rules. Signals on engines when double-headed.

28 One flag or light displayed where two are prescribed will indicate the same as two; but the proper display of all train signals is required. Indication of one flag or light.

29 When cars are pushed by an engine (except when shifting or making up trains in yards) a white light must be displayed on the front of the leading car. Light on leading car of cars pushed.

30 Each car on a passenger train must be connected with the engine by a communicating signal appliance. Air-whistle signal

31 A blue flag by day and a blue light by night, displayed at one or both ends of an engine, car or train, indicates that workmen are under or about it. When thus protected it must not be coupled to or moved. Workmen will display the blue signals and the same workmen are alone authorized to remove them. Other cars must not be placed on the same track so as to intercept the view of the blue signals, without first notifying the workmen. Car repairers' signal.

32 A green flag by day, and in addition a green light by night placed beside the track on the engineman's side, indicates that the track 3000 feet distant is in condition for speed of but six miles per hour, and the speed of a train will be controlled accordingly. Slow track.

A white flag by day, and, in addition, a white light by night, placed on the engineman's side at a point beyond the slow track, indicates that full speed may be resumed.

Slow-boards **33** A slow-board placed alongside the track reading "Reduce speed to — miles per hour" will indicate the rate of speed at which the track may be used at a point 3000 feet distant from such slow-board. The rate of speed indicated on the slow-board must not be exceeded. Beyond the point to be protected will be placed a sign reading "Resume full speed." Green lights and white lights respectively will be suspended by night from these boards.

Fixed Signals.

Placed. **34** Fixed signals are placed at drawbridges, junctions, stations, and other points that require special protection. Special instructions will be issued indicating their position and use.

Use of Signals.

Imperfect display or absence of usual signal. **35** A signal imperfectly displayed, or the absence of a signal at a place where a signal is usually shown, must be regarded as a stop signal and the fact reported to the Superintendent.

Acknowledging signal. **36** When a signal (except a fixed signal) is given to stop a train, it must be acknowledged, as prescribed by Rule 16 (*g*).

37 The engine-bell must be rung when an engine is about to move. Ringing of engine-bell.

38 The unnecessary use of either the whistle or the bell is prohibited. They will be used only as prescribed by rule or law, or to prevent accident. Use of whistle.

39 The whistle must not be sounded while passing a passenger train, except to prevent accident.

40 When a train passes a block station without markers, or in two or more parts, the towerman must notify block stations in rear and advance as provided in bell code. Trains without markers.

41 Towerman in advance block station must clear his signals, provided block in advance is clear, and display a white and a green flag by day, and a white and a green light by night, which is notification to the engineman that his train has parted.

42 Engineman shall answer with "train parted" signal.

43 At block stations where towerman is absent or incapacitated, so that instructions cannot be obtained, train must proceed to the next block as though caution card had been received, and conductor must report accordingly at the first telegraph block station or office. Towerman incapacitated.

Classification of Trains.

44 Trains of the first class are superior to those of the second; trains of the second class are superior to those of the third; and so on. Extra trains are inferior to regular trains. Superiority.

Direction. **45** All trains in the direction specified in the Time-table are superior to trains of the same class in the opposite direction.

12 hours late. **46** Regular trains twelve hours behind their schedule time lose both right and class, and can thereafter proceed only by train order.

Movement of Trains.

Starting signal. **47** A train must not start until the proper signal is given.

Not to depart in advance of time. **48** A train must not leave a station in advance of its schedule leaving time.

Delayed train. **49** A regular train which is delayed, and falls back on the time of another train of the same class, will proceed on its own schedule.

Work extras. **50** Work extras will be assigned working limits.

51 Work extras operating upon double track must move, within these limits, with the current of traffic, unless train orders otherwise direct.

Approaching end of double track, etc. **52** Trains must approach the end of double track, junctions, railroad crossings at grade, and drawbridges, prepared to stop, unless the switches and signals are right and the track is clear. Where required by law trains must stop.

Trains parting. **53** If a train should part while in motion, trainmen must use great care to prevent the detached parts from coming into collision. Enginemen must give the signal as provided in Rule 16 (*f*), and keep the front part of the train in motion until the detached portion is stopped, but if the engineman feels an application of air brakes indicating that train has broken between cars coupled with air, he should immediately shut off and put brake valve handle on lap to keep the two ends as near together as possible and thus reduce shock.

54 The front portion will have the right to go back, regardless of all trains, to recover the detached portion, first sending a flagman with danger signals **Ten Blocks** in the direction in which the train is to be backed, and running with great caution, at a speed not exceeding four miles per hour. On single tracks all the precautions required by the Rules must also be taken to protect the train against opposing trains. **The detached portion must not be moved or passed around until the front portion comes back,** except on written orders from the Train Dispatcher, which must not be given until he has received the acknowledgment for the order given to the forward portion.

55 An exception will only be made to the above when it is known that the detached portion has been stopped, and when the whole occurrence is in plain view, no curves or other obstructions intervening, so that signals can be seen from both portions of the train. In that event the conductor and engineman may arrange for the re-coupling, using the greatest caution.

56 On double track, the front portion must give the train-parted signal to trains running in the opposite direction. A train receiving this signal from a train on the opposite track must stop, and then proceed with caution until the detached portion of the train has been passed. When a train breaks down so it may obstruct the opposite track, trains on the opposite track must be stopped. On four tracks, enginemen will signal trains running in the opposite direction, and the conductor or flagman will signal trains running in the same direction.

57 If a south-bound passenger train should become detached, and the rear portion cannot be chained to the front portion without serious delay, the following will have strict observance :

58 Under no circumstances will the detached portion be pushed over the line.

59 The track occupied by the disabled train will be out of service until this train has cleared.

60 The Conductor of the disabled train will notify the Superintendent at once whether or not passengers can be transferred from the rear portion to the front portion.

61 Passengers will not be allowed to walk on the tracks.

62 If the occurrence takes place north of 96th Street, and a shop engine is available at Mott Haven Junction, orders will be issued to the shop train crew to proceed to the point where the disabled train is, and take the rear portion of the train to Mott Haven Yard, running it around the " Y," in order to get the engine on the south end of the train, and bring it to the Grand Central Station, except that when all the passengers have been transferred the empty cars must be left in the yards at Mott Haven.

63 If a shop engine is not available at Mott Haven, or a regular train is on the same track between the disabled train and the Junction, or if the occurrence takes place south of 96th Street, the front portion of the train will be brought to the Grand Central Station by the road engine, and switching crew and engine will be sent from the Grand Central Station for the detached portion.

64 If a north-bound passenger train should become detached the track occupied by the disabled train will be out of service until this train has cleared, and passengers must be transferred in accordance with instructions governing south-bound trains. The front portion of the train will be taken to Mott Haven Yard by the road engine, and shop train crew with an engine sent from that point to haul the rear portion to Mott Haven Yard, where the necessary changes and repairs will be made to the disabled train.

65 When a train is stopped by an accident or obstruction, the flagman must immediately go back with danger signals to insure full protection. At a point **six blocks** from the rear of his train he must place a torpedo on the rail; he must then continue to go back at least **ten blocks** from the rear of his train and place **another** torpedo on the rail, and must remain there until his train has passed out of the Flagmen.

section. When all is clear and he comes in, he will remove the torpedoes.

66 If the accident or obstruction occurs upon single track, or if it becomes necessary to protect the front of the train, or if any other track is obstructed, the fireman must go forward and use the same precautions. If the fireman is unable to leave the engine the forward trainman must be sent in his place.

67 When the flagman goes back to protect the rear of his train, the forward trainman must in the case of a passenger train, and the next trainman in the case of other trains, take his place on the train.

68 When necessary, the baggageman will take the place of the forward trainman.

69 When a train is detained at any of its usual stops more than **one** minute, or if it stops at an unusual point, the flagman must immediately go back as provided in Rule No. 65.

70 If for any cause the train moves at a slower rate of speed than usual, take such immediate action as may be necessary to protect it against following trains.

71 A flagman must always be stationed at the rear of every train, in either direction, between Grand Central Station and Mott Haven Junction, with danger signals ready for immediate use.

72 Unusual precaution must be taken in protecting the rear of trains in the Grand Central Station yard, especially in foggy weather. The rear trainman must remain on the rear platform of the rear car on trains leaving the Grand Central Station between the Station and the entrance to the tunnel, ready to protect his train at a moment's notice, in case of emergency.

73 On south-bound trains the rear trainman must be on the front platform of the rear car after leaving 55th Street, where he can look out for signals and assist in bringing the train into the Station. This does not in any way lessen the responsibility of the rear trainman in protecting his train if stopped in the yard.

74 Flagmen of south-bound trains left south of 72d Street, will walk to Grand Central Station, when their trains have cleared the section ahead. They will not be permitted to stop following trains (when it is no longer necessary for the protection of trains ahead) for the purpose of riding in.

75 When cars are pushed by an engine (except when shifting and making up trains in yards) a flagman must take a conspicuous position on the front of the leading car and signal the engineman in case of need.

76 If a train is stopped by a signal, in consequence of a disabled train being in the section, the towerman will give engineman and conductor a " detention card " informing them of the obstruction and authorizing them to proceed to the point of obstruction. They will then proceed cautiously into the section so occupied and render such assistance as may be necessary to move the disabled train and clear the section. This detention card must be shown to conductor of dis- Disabled train.

abled train, who, when ready to be moved, will allow following train to help his train as far as necessary. All operations of switching trains, cars, or engines, or of crossing from one track to another, must be performed only at such time and in such manner as to prevent the **chance** of accident, and strictly in accordance with the rules. Great caution must be used and good judgment is required to prevent unnecessary detention to trains, and Rule No. 65 must be strictly observed.

77 Should it become necessary, from any cause, for two or more trains to couple together and run as one train, they must not, under any circumstances, be separated on the line, except at a signal tower, and then only on written orders from the Train Dispatcher. In such cases the engineman of second train must notify operator and wait for signal from him to proceed.

Responsibility of conductors and enginemen.

78 Both conductors and enginemen are responsible for the safety of their trains and, under conditions not provided for by the rules, must take every precaution for their protection.

79 In all cases of doubt or uncertainty the safe course must be taken and no risks run.

RULES FOR
MOVEMENT BY TRAIN ORDERS.

RULES FOR
MOVEMENT BY TRAIN ORDERS.

80 For movements not provided for by Time-table, train orders will be issued by authority and over the signature of the Superintendent. They must contain neither information nor instructions not essential to such movements, and must be brief and clear; in the prescribed forms when applicable; and without erasure, alteration or interlineation. Train orders.

81 Each train order must be given in the same words to all persons or trains addressed.

82 Train orders will be numbered consecutively each day, beginning with No. 1 at midnight. Numbering.

83 Train orders must be addressed to those who are to execute them, naming the place at which each is to receive his copy. Those for a train must be addressed to the conductor and engineman, and also to any one who acts as its pilot. A copy for each person addressed must be supplied by the operator. To whom addressed.

84 Each train order must be written in full in a book provided for the purpose at the office of the Superintendent; and with it recorded the names of those who have signed for the order; the time and the signals which show when and from what offices the order was repeated and the responses transmitted; Record of train orders.

and the train dispatcher's initials. These records must be made at once, and never from memory or memoranda.

Identification. **85** Regular trains will be designated in train orders by their numbers, as "No. 10," or "2d No. 10," adding engine numbers if desired; extra trains by engine numbers, as "Extra 798," with the direction when necessary, as "North" or "South." Other numbers and time will be stated in figures only.

Signal "31" or "19." **86** To transmit a train order, the signal "31" or the signal "19" must be given to each office addressed, the number of copies being stated, if more or less than three—thus, "31 copy 5," or "19 copy 2."

Transmitting. **87** A train order to be sent to two or more offices must be transmitted simultaneously to as many of them as practicable. The several addresses must be in the order of superiority of trains, each office taking its proper address. When not sent simultaneously to all, the order must be sent first to the superior train.

Manifolding. **88** Operators receiving train orders must write them in manifold during transmission, and if they cannot at one writing make the requisite number of copies, must trace others from one of the copies first made.

"31" order. **89** When a "31" train order has been transmitted, operators must (unless otherwise directed) repeat it at once from the manifold copy in the succession in which the several offices have been addressed, and then write the time of repetition on the order. Each operator receiving the order should observe whether the others repeat correctly.

90 Those to whom the order is addressed, except enginemen, must then sign it, and the operator will send their signatures, preceded by the number of the order, to the Superintendent. The response "complete," and the time, with the initials of the Superintendent, will then be given by the train dispatcher. Each operator receiving this response will then write on each copy the word "complete," the time, and his last name in full, and then deliver a copy to each person addressed, except enginemen. Signatures.

91 The conductor must read his order aloud to the operator; the copy for each engineman must be delivered personally by the conductor, and the engineman must read it aloud to the conductor before proceeding.

92 When necessary to send an order to the meeting point, it must be stated in the body of the order accordingly. Order placed at meeting point.

93 When a "19" train order has been transmitted, operators must (unless otherwise directed) repeat it at once from the manifold copy, in the succession in which the several offices have been addressed. Each operator receiving the order should observe whether the others repeat correctly. When the order has been repeated correctly by an operator, the response "complete," and the time, with the initials of the Superin- "19" order.

NOTE.—In the movement of opposing trains, a "19" order must not be sent to the opposing train, the superiority of which is thereby restricted.

tendent, will be given by the train dispatcher. The operator receiving this response will then write on each copy the word "complete," the time, and his last name in full, and personally deliver a copy to each person addressed without taking his signature.

"X" response.

94 A train order may, when so directed by the train dispatcher, be acknowledged without repeating by the operator responding: "X; ___(Number of Train Order)___ to ___(Train Number)___," with the operator's initials and office signal. The operator must then write on the order his initials and the time.

"Complete" not to be given until "X" response received.

95 "Complete" must not be given to a train order for delivery to an inferior train until the order has been repeated or the "X" response sent by the operator who receives the order for the superior train.

"X" response given before "Complete" is received.

96 When a train order has been repeated or "X" response sent, and before "complete" has been given, the order must be treated as a holding order for the train addressed, but must not be otherwise acted on until "complete" has been given.

Failure of line.

97 If the line fails before an office has repeated an order or has sent the "X" response, the order at that office is of no effect and must be there treated as if it had not been sent.

Preserve lowest copy.

98 The operator who receives and delivers a train order must preserve the lowest copy.

Orders delivered by dispatcher.

99 For train orders delivered by the train dispatcher the requirements as to the record and delivery are the same as at other offices, and such orders shall be first written in manifold, so as to leave an impression in the record book, from which transmission shall be made.

100 A train order to be delivered to a train at a point not a telegraph station, or at one at which the telegraph office is closed, must be addressed to **Delivery of order at non-telegraph station.**

" *C. and E.* ——— (*at* ———), *care of* ———,"

and forwarded and delivered by the conductor or other person in whose care it is addressed. When Form 31 is used "complete" will be given upon the signature of the person by whom the order is to be delivered, who must be supplied with copies for the conductor and engineman addressed, and a copy upon which he shall take their signatures. This copy he must deliver to the first operator accessible, who must preserve it, and at once transmit the signatures of the conductor and engineman to the train dispatcher.

Orders so delivered must be acted on as if "complete" had been given in the usual way.

For orders which are sent, in the manner herein provided, to a train, the superiority of which is thereby restricted, "complete" must not be given to an inferior train until the signatures of the conductor and engineman of the superior train have been sent to the Superintendent.

101 When a train is named in a train order, all its sections are included unless particular sections are specified, and each section included must have copies addressed and delivered to it. **Sections of trains.**

102 Unless otherwise directed, an operator must not repeat or give the "X" response to a train order for **"X" response.**

a train, the engine of which has passed his train-order signal, until he has ascertained that the conductor and engineman have been notified that he has orders for them.

Duration of orders. **103** Train orders once in effect continue so until fulfilled, superseded or annulled. Any part of an order specifying a particular movement may be either superseded or annulled.

Orders held by or issued for a regular train become void when such train loses both right and class as prescribed by Rules 6, and 46, or is annulled.

Train-order signal. **104** A fixed signal must be used at each train-order office, which shall indicate "stop" when trains are to be stopped for train orders. When there are no orders the signal must indicate "proceed."

Display of train-order signal. **105** When an operator receives the signal "31," or "19," he must immediately display the "stop signal" and then reply "stop displayed"; and until the orders have been delivered or annulled the signal must not be restored to "proceed."

Handsignals. **106** Operators must have the proper appliances for hand signaling ready for immediate use if the fixed signal should fail to work properly. If a signal is not displayed at a night office, trains which have not been notified must stop and ascertain the cause, and report the facts to the Superintendent from the next open telegraph office.

Reporting trains. **107** Operators will promptly record and report to the Superintendent the time of departure of all trains and the direction of extra trains. They will record the time of arrival of trains and report it when so directed.

108 The following signs and abbreviations may be used: Signs and abbreviations.

Initials for signature of the Superintendent.

Such office and other signals as are arranged by the Superintendent.

C & E—for Conductor and Engineman.

X—Train will be held until order is made "complete."

Com—for Complete.

O S—Train Report.

No—for Number.

Eng—for Engine.

Sec—for Section.

Psgr—for Passenger.

Frt—for Freight.

Mins—for Minutes.

Jct—for Junction.

Dispr—for Train Dispatcher.

Opr—for Operator.

31 or 19—to clear the line for train orders, and for operators to ask for train orders.

S D—for "Stop Displayed."

The usual abbreviations for the names of the months and stations.

FORMS OF TRAIN ORDERS.

FORMS OF TRAIN ORDERS.

Form A.—Fixing Meeting Points for Opposing Trains.

(1) ——— will meet ——— at ———.

(2) ——— will meet ——— at ——— ——— at ——— (and so on).

EXAMPLES.

(1) *No.* 1 *will meet No.* 2 *at Bombay.*
No. 3 *will meet* 2*d No.* 4 *at Siam.*
No. 5 *will meet Extra* 95 *at Hongkong.*
Extra 652 *North will meet Extra* 231 *South at Yokohama.*

(2) *No.* 1 *will meet No.* 2 *at Bombay;* 2*d No.* 4 *at Siam; and Extra* 95 *at Hongkong.*

Trains receiving these orders will run with respect to each other to the designated points and there meet in the manner provided by the Rules.

Form B. Extra Trains.

(1) Eng —— will run extra —— to ——.

(2) Eng —— will run extra —— to —— and return to ——.

EXAMPLE.

(1) *Eng* 99 *will run extra Berber to Gaza.*

(2) *Eng* 99 *will run extra Berber to Gaza and return to Cabul.*

A train receiving this order is not required to protect itself against opposing extra trains, unless directed by order to do so, but must keep clear of all regular trains, as required by rule.

(3) Eng —— will run extra leaving —— on —— as follows with right over all trains.

Leave ——.
" ——.
Arrive ——.

EXAMPLE.

(3) *Eng* 77 *will run extra leaving Turin on Thursday Feb.* 17*th as follows with right over all trains.*

Leave Turin 11.30 *p.m.*
" *Pekin* 12.25 *a.m.*
" *Canton* 1.47 *a.m.*
Arrive Rome 2.22 *a.m.*

This order may be varied by specifying the kind of extra and the particular trains over which the extra shall or shall not have the right. Trains over which the extra is thus given the right must clear the time of the extra five (5) minutes.

Form C.—Work Extra.

(1) Work extra —— will work —— until —— between —— and ——.

EXAMPLES.

(1) *Work extra* 292 *will work* 7 *a.m. until* 6 *p.m. between Berne and Turin.*

The working limits should be as short as practicable, to be changed as the progress of the work may require. The above may be combined, thus:

(*a*) *Work extra* 292 *will run Berne to Turin and work* 7 *a.m. until* 6 *p.m. between Turin and Rome.*

When an order has been given to "work" between designated points, no other extra shall be authorized to run over that part of the track without provision for passing the work extra.

When it is anticipated that a work extra may be where it cannot be reached for orders, it may be directed to report for orders at a given time and place, or an order may be given that it shall clear the track for (or protect itself after a certain hour against) a designated extra by adding to (1) the following words:

(*b*) *And will keep clear of* (*or protect against*) *Extra* 223 *south between Antwerp and Brussels after* 2.10 *p.m.*

In this case, extra 223 must not pass the northernmost point before 2.10 p.m., at which time the work extra must be out of the way, or protected (as the order may require) between those points.

When the movement of an extra over the working limits cannot be anticipated by these or other orders to the work extra, an order must be given to such extra, to protect itself against the work extra, in the following form:

(*c*) *Extra* 76 *will protect against Work Extra* 95 *between Lyons and Paris.*

This may be added to the order to run extra.

A work extra when met or overtaken by an extra must allow it to pass.

When it is desirable that a work extra shall at all

times protect itself while on working limits, it may be done by adding to (1) the following words:

(*d*) *protecting itself.*

A train receiving this order must, whether standing or moving, protect itself within the working limits in both directions in the manner prescribed by Rule 65.

Whenever an extra is given orders to run over working limits it must at the same time be given a copy of the order sent to the work extra.

To enable a work extra to work upon the time of a regular train, the following form may be used:

(*e*) *Work Extra* 292 *will protect against No.* 55 *between Berne and Turin.*

A train receiving this order will work upon the time of the train mentioned in the order, and protect itself against it as prescribed by Rule 65.

The regular train receiving this order must run, expecting to find the work extra protecting itself within the limits named.

Form D.— Holding Order.

Hold —— at ——.

EXAMPLES.

(1) *Hold No.* 2 *at Berlin.*

(2) *Hold all east-bound trains at Berlin.*

This order will be addressed to the operator and acknowledged in the usual manner. It must be respected by conductors and enginemen of trains thereby directed to be held as if addressed to them.

When a train has been so held it must not proceed

until the order to hold is annulled, or an order given to the operator in the form:

"—— *may go.*"

Form D will only be used when necessary to hold trains until orders can be given, or in case of emergency.

Form E.—Annulling a Regular Train.

(1) —— of —— is annulled —— to ——.

(2) —— due to leave —— —— is annulled —— to ——.

EXAMPLES.

(1) *No.* 1 *of Feb.* 29 *is annulled Alaska to Halifax.*

(2) *No.* 3, *due to leave Naples Saturday, Feb.* 29, *is annulled Alaska to Halifax.*

The train annulled loses both right and class between the stations named, and must not be restored under its original number between those stations.

Form F.—Annulling an Order.

" Order No. —— is annulled."

If an order which is to be annulled has not been delivered to a train, the annulling order will be addressed to the operator, who will destroy all copies of the order annulled but his own, and write on that:

Annulled by Order No. ——.

EXAMPLE.

Order No. 10 *is annulled.*

An order which has been annulled must not be reissued under its original number.

In the address of an order annulling another order, the train first named must be that to which right was given by the order annulled, and when the order is not transmitted simultaneously to all concerned, it must be first sent to the point at which that train is to receive it and the required response made, before the order is sent for other trains.

Form G.—Annulling Part of an Order.

That part of Order No. —— reading —— is annulled.

EXAMPLE.

That part of Order No. 10 *reading* "*No.* 1 *will meet No.* 2 *at Sparta*" *is annulled.*

In the address of an order annulling a part of an order, the train first named must be that to which right was given by the part annulled, and when the order is not transmitted simultaneously to all concerned, it must be first sent to the point at which that train is to receive it, and the required response made, before the order is sent for other trains.

Form H.—Superseding an Order or a Part of an Order.

This order will be given by adding to prescribed forms the words "instead of ——."

(1) —— will meet —— at —— instead of ——.

(2) —— has right over —— —— to —— instead of ——.

(3) —— will display signals for —— —— to —— instead of ——.

EXAMPLES.

(1) *No. 1 will meet No. 2 at Hongkong instead of Bombay.*

(2) *No. 1 has right over No. 2 Mecca to Medina instead of Mirbat.*

(3) *No. 1 will display signals for Eng 85 Astrakhan to Teheran instead of Cabul.*

An order which has been superseded must not be reissued under its original number.

Form I.—Providing for a Movement Against the Current of Traffic.

—— has right over opposing trains on —— track —— to ——.

EXAMPLE.

(1) *No. 4 has right over opposing trains on No. 2 (or westward) track Mecca to Mirbat.*

A train must not be moved against the current of traffic until the track on which it is to run has been cleared of opposing trains.

Under this order the first named train must use the track specified between the two points named, and has the right over opposing trains on that track between those points. Opposing trains must not leave the point last named until the first named train arrives.

An inferior train between the points named moving with the current of traffic in the same direction as the first named train must receive a copy of the order, and may then proceed on its schedule, or right.

This order may be modified as follows:

(2) After —— arrives at —— —— has right over opposing trains on —— track —— to ——.

EXAMPLE.

After No. 1 arrives at Mecca No. 4 has right over opposing trains on No. 2 (or westward) track Mecca to Mirbat.

Under (2) the train to be moved against the current of traffic must not leave the first named point until the arrival of the first named train.

When practicable, trains with the current of traffic must receive the order at one station distant from the last named station; when it cannot be done, mention must be made in the body of the order.

Form J.—Providing for the Use of a Section of Double Track as Single Track.

—— track will be used as single track between —— and ——.

If it is desired to limit the time for such use add (from —— until ——).

EXAMPLE.

No. 2 (or westward) track will be used as single track between Mecca and Mirbat.

Adding if desired

from 1 p.m. until 3 p.m.

Under this order all trains must use the track specified between the stations named, and will be governed by rules for single track.

Trains running against the current of traffic on the track named must be clear of the track at the expiration of the time named, or protected as prescribed by Rule 65.

HARLEM LINE.

CAUTION CARD.

FOR CLOSING UP TRAINS IN SECTION.

____________*Tower*,____________*190*________________*M.*

To Engineer and Conductor,

____________*Train* (*or Engine*)____________*on*____________*track.*

Pull up slowly into next section, regardless of fixed signals, close to the preceding train.

____
Operator.

NOTE.—The engineer receiving this card, duly dated, timed and signed, will run to the next signal or point of obstruction with train under *full control* and as he knows the way to be clear, and on completion of the trip will send the card to this office.

____
Superintendent.

HARLEM LINE.

No. ____________

CLEARANCE CARD.

____________ *Tower* ____________ *190* ____________ *M.*

To Conductor and Engineer,

Train No. ____________ *on Track No.* ____________

Signal has failed to clear: proceed with caution to next signal tower.

____

Operator.

This card must not be used except in case of failure of block signals, *and* when section has been duly reported clear by the operator at advance tower. The engineer receiving it duly dated, timed and signed, will run to next signal with train under *full control,* and on completion of trip will send the card to this office.

____

Superintendent.

HARLEM LINE.

TRAIN DETENTION SERVICE.

__________*Tower*__________*190*____ __________*M.*

*To Conductor and Engineer, No.*__________*Street:*

__________*Train*__________*is stalled (or disabled) at*__________*Street.*

Pull slowly into next section, *regardless of fixed signals, to disabled train, and help*

*them to*__________

Superintendent.

__________*Conductor.*

__________*Engineer.* __________*Operator.*

This card must not be used except in case of train being stalled or disabled. The Conductor and Engineer receiving it duly dated, timed and signed, will run as per order herein given, and on completion of trip will send the card to this office.

____

Superintendent.

GRAND CENTRAL STATION AND HARLEM LINE.

OFFICE OF THE SUPERINTENDENT.

*New York*______________*190*__

*Telegraphic Train Order Number*________

*To*____________________________

*At*______________

*Rec'd*______________*M.* ______________ *Superintendent.*

*Made*______________ *By*______________ *Dispatcher.*

*at*______________*M.*

*Received by*____________________________*Operator.*

Rules for Reporting Accidents.

109 All accidents, no matter how trivial they may appear, occurring at the Grand Central Station, or on the Harlem Line, must be reported promptly by wire. Prompt report.

110 Whenever an accident occurs resulting in personal injuries, a written report must be made to the Superintendent, giving all the facts obtainable, and as soon thereafter as possible a regular report filled out complete must be forwarded to the Superintendent's Office.

111 State on the blank in each case whether the injured person was an employe, passenger, or an outsider.

112 In giving the names of witnesses, bear in mind that any persons who were at or near the scene of the accident are classed as witnesses, and even though they may have no knowledge of the occurrence, or did not actually see it, still their names may be essential to the proper protection of the company's interests. Witnesses.

113 When an employe is an eye-witness of an accident, even though the duty of making a report does not devolve upon him, he will bring the matter to the attention of the proper official, giving all the information he may be able to secure.

114 If an accident occurs resulting in personal injuries, damage to clothing, etc., by persons falling on or from platforms or bridges, a careful examination of the premises must be made at once to ascertain Platforms and bridges.

the actual cause of the accident; whether refuse was responsible for the fall, or whether or not the platform or bridge was wet or slippery from water, snow, ice or grease.

Snow and Ice. **115** If fall was due to accumulation of snow and ice, the date and time snow began to fall,—ceased to fall, work of removal of same was commenced, and date and time the platform or bridge was in safe condition for use, must be given in space provided for that purpose.

Obstructions. **116** If an accident occurs resulting in personal injuries, damage to clothing, etc., by reason of an obstruction on or near tracks, platforms or bridges, it will be necessary to ascertain how long such obstruction existed, and by whose authority it was allowed to exist. Was it properly reported when first noticed?

Repairs. **117** If the premises where an accident occurred were undergoing repairs, so advise, stating who was in charge of the work and responsible for giving warning and proper protection.

Vehicles. **118** If accidents occur in which wagons are involved, the name and address of the owner and driver, and the extent of damage done and injury received must be given.

Damage equipment. **119** If accidents occur resulting in damage to equipment or to other property of the Companies terminating at this Station, the cause of the accident, and name in full of the party at fault, must be given, as well as all other information called for on the blank.

Inspection. **120** Proper inspection must be made of all points where accidents occur, that actual facts may be contained in the report.

121 In case of a disabled train requiring assistance, the conductor will notify the Superintendent's Office at once on the N. Y. C. & H. R. R. R. form 111, Telegraphic Report of Accident, from the nearest signal tower, bearing in mind that his first thought should be for the comfort of passengers. Written report on regular Harlem Line Accident blank must be forwarded to the Superintendent's Office as soon thereafter as possible. Disabled train.

SPECIAL RULES.

SPECIAL RULES.

Train Masters.

122 Train Masters report to and receive their instructions from the Superintendent. Report to.

123 Pass the required examination as to character, habits, education, and record of previous service. Knowledge of Time-tables, rules and regulations, characteristics of road, grades, curves, etc., location and indication of all fixed signals, construction and use of air brake appliances. How to meet emergencies and break-downs; also for color perception, strength of vision and hearing. Examination.

124 It is their duty to exercise general supervision over all employes in Train and Yard service on their respective districts; to know that they fully understand and observe the rules; and to see that no employe is allowed in train service without having passed the prescribed examination. Duty.

125 Give special attention to the prompt and regular movement of traffic; see that the proper number of cars are moved by each engine; that no more shop trains are run than actually necessary; watch and investigate the detention of trains; be familiar with the proper distribution of cars, and make frequent inspection of bulletin boards and be responsible for their condition. Movement traffic.

Accidents. **126** In case of accident, when necessary, proceed to the place, take general charge of clearing the road, and protect the wrecked property, unless otherwise provided for.

Other duties. **127** Perform such other duties as may be assigned you by the Superintendent.

Chief Train Dispatchers.

Report to. **128** Chief Train Dispatchers report to and receive their instructions from the Superintendent.

Supervision over. **129** They will have charge of Train Dispatchers and telegraph operators on their respective districts or divisions.

Duty. **130** See that train orders are issued in accordance with the prescribed forms, go over the division as often as convenient, and give special attention to the condition of instruments, wires, and train order signals, and prevent unnecessary use of the wires.

131 See that only one person issues train orders over the same territory at the same time.

Rules for Train Dispatchers.

Report to. **132** Report to and receive instructions from the Chief Train Dispatcher.

133 Pass the examination required as to:

Examination. Character, habits, education and record of previous service.

Knowledge of Time-table, rules and regulations.

Characteristics of road, grades, curves, sidings, etc.

Location and indication of all fixed signals.

Report for duty promptly, and remain until relieved; when relieved, make, with ink, in the train order book, a written transfer of all orders issued and not fully executed; see that all such orders, and everything pertaining thereto, are fully understood by the relieving dispatcher.

134 Report to the operator at Mott Haven Junction departure of all trains or engines. Trains or engines arriving on the Harlem line at Mott Haven Junction must be reported promptly to the Dispatcher, giving class of train, number of cars, and road to which it belongs. Records.

135 Keep in a book, provided for that purpose, all instructions and train orders which may from time to time be issued to operators and others; also a record of all failures of signals.

136 When the line is obstructed, and it becomes necessary to use "Single Track" over any portion of it, trains will be moved by telegraph. The nature of the order given must be understood perfectly by the Conductor and Engineman of the train to whom it is addressed, and they must not proceed with their train until they have sent their understanding of the order and received in reply from the person sending such order the words "All Right," with his signature attached. Single track.

137 Conform to all the rules and regulations for the movement of trains by train orders. Duty.

Orders.

138 Issue orders for the movement of trains in the name of the Superintendent.

139 Use the simplest form of orders that will accomplish the desired result, and limit the number of specified movements in each order as far as practicable.

140 Use care in sending train orders; do not transmit an order faster than the receiving operator can take and write plainly.

141 Watch the movement of trains; anticipate as far as possible and prevent unnecessary delays.

Records.

142 Keep a record showing the time of arrival and departure of trains at all towers; see that operators report trains promptly. File the records for future reference.

143 Keep a record of the important incidents that occur during your hours of duty, that affect the movement of, or endanger trains, and in sufficient detail to give all necessary information whenever called for. Report such cases to the Chief Train Dispatcher.

144 See that the operators carefully observe the rules for movement of trains by train orders, and that they perform their duty with promptness. Report any who are in any way careless or inaccurate.

Trains running single track.

145 When necessary to give extra trains in opposite directions, on single track, running orders to the same point, specify in the orders how they shall pass.

Standard time.

146 See that nothing is allowed to interfere with the transmission of standard time at the prescribed hour.

Telegraph Operators and Towermen.

147 Telegraph Operators report to and receive their orders from the Chief Train Dispatcher, and will comply with the instructions of the Superintendent. Report to.

148 Pass the examination required as to:

Character, habits, education, and record of previous service.

Knowledge of Time-table, rules and regulations.

Also, for color perception, strength of vision and hearing.

149 Give exclusive attention to the business of the company during the prescribed hours.

150 Must have a thorough knowledge of switch-boards and their manipulation, all wires leading into their office, all instruments used in telegraphing and the care and maintenance of necessary batteries. Knowledge of switch-boards, etc.

151 When required will be in the offices at other than regular office hours in case of accident or emergency, or whenever the interests of the company require.

152 Day operators are managers of their respective offices unless otherwise directed. Managers.

153 Where both day and night operators are employed, do not leave the office until relieved by each other. Relieve each other.

154 Consider the telegraph a confidential service, and treat the contents of messages which are sent, received, or overheard accordingly. Confidential service.

Students. **155** No students will be allowed in offices without the written approval of the Superintendent.

Private lines. **156** Do not allow private lines or instruments on the company's premises, except as authorized by the Superintendent.

Train orders. **157** Be familiar with the "Rules for the movement of trains by train orders," and know that required signals are promptly displayed; see that all orders received are properly delivered, and that no order is accepted for delivery to a train that has passed, or for delivery to a train that has received a clearance card at your station.

158 Be ready at all times to receive train orders, and when relieved, transfer to the relieving operator all train orders, notices, and messages on hand.

159 Copy all train orders on the blanks provided for that purpose.

Delivery messages. **160** Give immediate attention to the delivery of messages affecting in any way the safety of trains or the property of the company. When unable to personally deliver them promptly to the parties addressed, call on any employe to make the delivery, and inform him of the importance of the message.

Date and file. **161** Messages must be correctly dated and show the time filed, the time sent or received, and the private signals and office calls of the sending and receiving operators.

Reports. **162** Report the departure of all trains to the dispatcher promptly, unless otherwise instructed.

163 Operators at East 72d Street tower will report by wire to 50th Street all Southbound extra trains.

164 Use great care in adjusting instruments at all times, and especially in bad weather, never opening the key unless positive that wire is not being used. **Adjustment.**

165 Observe all interruptions to circuits, and make frequent examinations of all office connections, viz.: at switchboards, relays, keys underneath the table, and at lightning arresters or any other devices in circuit with the wires. **Examine instruments.**

166 Should the circuit remain open at any time over two minutes apply the ground wire and report promptly to the next testing office, or to the Chief Train Dispatcher, which way the wire is open. The ground wire must not be used except for testing wires when interrupted, and then only long enough to report or to transact unusually important business; when the latter is done the Test Operator must be advised that ground has been so used. **Ground wire.**

167 Make such wire connections on switchboards and such wire tests as directed to do by the Test Operator, and respect his signal and obey his instructions promptly. When directed by the Test Operator to open or ground a wire do not fail to reply, "Now," immediately upon doing so. Must not make any wire connections unless directed to do so, and must always keep an instrument on the wire on which directions are being given until the desired communication is restored. **Tests.**

Unnecessary use of wire. **168** Unnecessary communication on the wire between operators is forbidden.

Messages to be handled. **169** Messages, unless on company's business, or signed by some officer of the company or its immediate connections, must be refused.

Unnecessary use of wire. **170** When messages are offered for transmission which could apparently go by train mail, call the attention of the person signing the message to the fact and, if still so requested, transmit the message, sending a copy by mail to the Superintendent for investigation.

Contention for circuit. **171** Contention for circuit, or the use of profane or indecent language on the circuit, will not be permitted.

Speed of sending operators. **172** In transmitting messages regulate the speed to suit the ability of the receiving operator. Under ordinary circumstances the sending operator will be held responsible for errors in transmission.

Sign office call. **173** Sign own office call after every third call. After calling an office nine times, yield to any other office wanting the circuit.

To retain circuit. **174** Circuit can be retained by saying "HR" after the signature to a message and before signing office call; but this will not prevent taking the business of any office after sending to it, owing to the fact that he has business for other offices. The key must never be thrown open to hold the circuit.

Personal signal. **175** Do not change personal signal without permission from the Chief Train Dispatcher, or other person in charge of operators on the division.

176 Give personal attention to the care of the clock in the office; have a regular time for winding it. Report to the dispatcher any daily variations of over a minute from the time given by the standard. Clock.

177 Towermen are enjoined to observe trains passing their block stations very closely, and should anything be wrong to notify block station in advance. Observe trains closely.

178 Telegraph Numerals.

1 Wait a minute.
3 Give me correct time.
4 Where shall I repeat from?
5 Close your key; you are breaking.
7 I have business; are you ready?
8 Busy on other wire.
9 To clear the line for train orders, and for operators to ask for train orders.
12 How do you understand?
13 Understand.
14 What is the weather?
15 Have you any orders?
18 What is the matter?
19 Train order—as provided in the rules governing same.
21 Extreme emergency. This must have preference over all other business except "9" "19" "31" and "39".
23 The following is for you and others.
24 Repeat this back.

28 Do you get my writing?

29 This is private and must be delivered in sealed envelope.

31 Train order — as provided in the rules governing same.

34 This message is of great importance.

39 This must have preference over all other business and used **only** by the Manager.

92 This message should be copied in ink.

The word "wire" will be used by the Testing Operator for wire-testing purposes, and will have preference over all signals excepting "9," ("19" "31" and "39," as provided in the rules).

NOTE.— Operators must not make use of any signals for business other than that to which such signals are ascribed.

Rules for Levermen.

Report.

179 Levermen in Towers Nos. 1 and 2 will report to and receive instructions from the director, except as otherwise ordered.

Examination.

180 Pass the examination required as to:

Character, habits, education, and record of previous service, knowledge of Time-tables, rules and regulations, characteristics of yard.

Location and indication of all yard signals.

Color perception, strength of vision and hearing.

Call routes.

181 The director must call the routes plainly, and leverman will repeat the instructions before taking any action.

Rules for Yard-masters.

182 Report to and receive instructions from the Train-master. Report to.

183 Pass the examination required as to : Examination.

Character, habits, education and record of previous service.

Knowledge of Time-table, rules and regulations.

Construction and use of air brake appliances.

Also, for color perception, strength of vision, and hearing.

184 Will have charge of the yard and see that same is kept in good order; be responsible for the prompt movement, proper distribution and placing of cars so that they may be inspected or repaired.

185 See that trains are properly made up and leave on time, reporting all detentions and causes of same.

186 Care must be taken so that unnecessary noise will not be made with engines or by employes when near sleeping cars in service.

187 Keep a record of the initials, number and seals of each freight car arriving at or departing from the yard, giving date and train numbers, and make daily reports of the same on the blanks provided for that purpose. Records.

188 Freight cars must not be forwarded unless accompanied by memorandum bills; such memorandums specifying contents must show to whose order cars are billed at Melrose Jct. Waybill freight cars

Unfit for duty. **189** Do not permit a train to start with an engineman, conductor or trainman who has apparently been drinking intoxicating liquors, or is unfit for duty, nor fail to report such occurrences at once to the trainmaster.

190 Be familiar with the rules for movement of trains and for the government of employes in the train and yard service, and require the prompt and efficient discharge of duty by all employes subject to your direction.

Bulletin boards. **191** See that all official orders and notices are kept posted on bulletin boards provided for that purpose.

Noise. **192** See that no unnecessary noise is made with engines or by employes in doing their work.

Rules for Station Masters.

Report to. **193** Report to and receive instructions from the Superintendent; obey all orders or instructions issued by the several officers of the Company relating to the business of their respective departments.

Examination. **194** Pass the examination as to:

Character, habits, education and record of previous service.

Knowledge of Time-table, rules and regulations.

Also, for color perception, strength of vision and hearing.

Duty. **195** Devote your time exclusively to the business of the company, unless expressly exempted in writing by the Superintendent from so doing.

196 Give prompt attention to all correspondence relating to the business of the company. Correspondence.

197 Avoid giving offense and act with the view of accommodating the public and promoting the best interests of the company, notifying the Superintendent or heads of departments interested of anything prejudicial thereto, or conducive to its good, present or prospective.

198 Be responsible for the company's property, including station buildings and grounds, and for the care and safety of all property intrusted to the company in the transaction of its business, and for the prompt and efficient discharge of duty by all employes subject to your direction.

199 Preserve order in and about the stations; keep the buildings and grounds connected therewith neat and clean and in proper condition for the accommodation of passengers. Order.

200 Care must be taken to keep the waiting-room and other parts of the building clean and free from rubbish, sweepings, hot ashes, and all inflammable material.

201 Cleaning of cars, except a light dusting, will not be permitted in the station. Papers and other refuse must not be thrown out on the tracks or platforms, but must be put in boxes provided for that purpose. Cleaning.

202 Subject to the Superintendent, regulate the places where hacks and other vehicles shall be allowed to stand, and where the drivers thereof and persons representing hotels, or other persons not in the em- Vehicles ploy of the company, shall remain while on the company's premises.

Articles for sale. **203** Do not allow unauthorized persons to offer any articles whatever for sale on the company's property.

Advertisements. **204** Do not permit advertisements of any kind except such as are duly authorized by the Superintendent to be posted on the company's premises.

Loiterers. **205** Do not allow loiterers or disorderly persons to interfere with the comfort and convenience of passengers or with employes in the performance of their duties.

Make-up of trains. **206** See that passenger trains are made up in the order designated, that crews report for duty at the prescribed hour, and that trains leave on time.

Uniforms. **207** Inspect the uniforms of employes and know that they are presentable.

Announcement. **208** Before the arrival or departure of a train announce in the waiting-room, and on the platform, its direction, its destination, state whether local or through, and mention the next and principal stops.

(This duty may be delegated to doormen or ushers.)

Keep proper records. **209** Keep a record of all trains and cars, note all irregularities, and see that reports of same are made to the proper officer.

Unfit for duty. **210** Do not permit a train to start with an engineman, conductor or trainman who has apparently been drinking intoxicating liquors, or is unfit for duty, nor fail to report such occurrences at once to the Superintendent.

211 Employes on duty or in uniform will not be allowed to occupy seats in the waiting-rooms or loiter in or about the Station, except in the rooms provided for them. Employes Loitering.

Station Agents.

212 Station Agents report to and receive their orders from the Superintendent, and will comply with instructions issued by the Passenger, Freight, and Accounting Departments. Report to.

213 Will have charge of the business of the company at the station, all property connected therewith, and all persons employed thereat. Duty.

214 See that the station and grounds are in proper condition for the safety, comfort and convenience of patrons. Condition of premises.

215 See that the station is supplied with the necessary lanterns, flags, and torpedoes, and that they are ready for immediate use. Signal appliances.

216 Do not permit advertising matter to be posted in or about stations, or other structures located on the company's property, without proper authority. Advertising matter.

217 Enforce order, and require all persons employed at the station to be polite and considerate in their intercourse with the public. Order and politeness.

218 Use every proper means to secure and hold traffic for the road. Hold traffic.

219 Open the ticket office thirty minutes before the departure of trains, and, as far as possible, see that passengers have tickets before boarding trains. Sale of tickets.

220 Do not sell tickets to persons who are not in condition to care for themselves (unless accompanied by an attendant), or whose conduct may be a source of annoyance or danger to other passengers.

Printed information for public. **221** Post, in a prominent place, Time-tables and Tariffs, and other matter issued by the Freight and Passenger Departments for the information of the public.

Hacks, etc. **222** Designate the place where hacks, omnibuses, and other vehicles, the drivers thereof, and persons representing hotels, may remain while on the company's property.

Trucks. **223** Baggage and express trucks must not be left where they are liable to be pushed or blown onto the tracks, or to come in contact with passengers. They must not be wheeled alongside a train from which passengers are alighting, and, when not in use, must be kept in the places assigned for them.

U. S. Mail. **224** Employes must use the utmost care in looking after the U. S. mails. They must not be left unguarded for a single moment, nor allowed to remain on the platform where they will be liable to get wet or be tampered with, nor must they be left where passengers may fall over them. They must be kept carefully under lock and key unless some one is in charge of them, or until such time as they are delivered to the person authorized to receive them.

Legal papers **225** When legal papers are served on agents as representatives of the company, agents will note thereon the date, hour, and by whom served, and forward papers at once to the General Counsel at New

York by U. S. mail, and inform the Superintendent by wire of the serving of the papers and their object.

Rules for Doormen.

226 They will report to and receive instructions from the Station Master, and must not be absent from duty without permission. Report to.

227 Remain in places to which they are assigned, and do not read newspapers or books while on duty. Reading.

228 Always be courteous to passengers and refrain from any altercation. Whenever a dispute with passengers is imminent, do not offer any remarks beyond referring them to the Station Master's office. Avoid altercation.

229 Do not allow passengers to take large bundles into the trains, entailing inconvenience to other passengers. Large bundles.

230 Do not allow employes, or encourage other persons, to stand or loiter around the gates while admitting passengers to trains, but devote your time to seeing that passengers have tickets and are directed to the right train. Loitering.

Rules for Attendants.

231 They will report to and receive instructions from the Station Master, except as otherwise instructed. Report to.

232 Do not read newspapers or books while on duty, but give your whole attention to caring for passengers. Reading on duty.

Assist passengers. **233** Be on the alert continually to assist patrons; any discrimination will be considered just cause for dismissal.

234 Assist passengers with luggage to and from trains; soliciting for tips will not be permitted.

235 As soon as passengers have been cared for, immediately offer their services to others, if there are any in waiting who may be in need of help. Do not loiter around a cab or carriage after the patrons have been cared for.

Station Baggage Masters.

Report to. **236** Station Baggage Master report to and receive orders from the Superintendent or Station Agent, as directed, and will comply with instructions issued by the General Baggage Agent.

Duty. **237** Will have charge of the baggage-room and persons employed therein.

238 Be responsible for baggage while in your charge.

239 See that all baggage is handled carefully, and be civil and obliging to passengers.

240 See that no unauthorized person has access to the baggage-room.

Rules for Baggagemen.

Report to. **241** Report to and receive instructions from the Station Baggage Master.

242 Pass the examination required as to: Examination.
Character, habits, education, and record of previous service.

243 Be respectful and courteous at all times to passengers, cheerfully giving all necessary information concerning transportation of baggage. Passengers.

244 Do not receive for transportation any article except the company's material and supplies, unless duly authorized by the rules and orders. Carry no letters, valuable parcels, or money packages, except on railroad business. Articles for transportation.

245 Take great care in the handling and delivery of United States mail, and see that it is regularly received from and delivered to the proper agents, and strictly conform to all regulations pertaining to the mail service, promptly reporting every irregularity. U. S. Mail.

Rules for Baggage Elevatormen.

246 They will report to and receive instructions from the Foreman of Elevators. Report to.

247 Pass the examination required as to: Examination.
Character, habits, record of previous service.
Vision and hearing.

248 Will be held responsible for the proper operation of the elevators, and must not permit anyone except the repairmen or proper official to operate same. Duty.

249 Employes and all others are forbidden to lounge around the elevators, and all concerned are Danger elevator shafts.

cautioned in regard to the danger existing in looking down the elevator shafts.

Trucks. **250** All trucks must be located on the platform of each elevator so that the ends do not come in contact with the sides of the shaft.

251 Porters will not be permitted to block the exit by baggage or trucks, and must use the utmost dispatch consistent with safety in performing their duties.

Care to avoid accidents. **252** All employes must exercise caution in order to prevent accidents to persons or damage to baggage occurring, and especial care must be taken to avoid accidents on account of elevator gates ascending or descending.

Protecting passengers from elevator walls. **253** In addition to other duties, you will, when passengers are being discharged from incoming trains keep a sharp lookout to protect them from coming in contact with the walls of the elevator shaft, giving sufficient warning of such danger.

Reading. **254** Reading while on duty is forbidden.

Bell code. **255** The bell code outlined below will be the only recognized signals, and the elevatorman will not move the elevators except upon proper signal, or unless authorized to do so by orders of the proper official. All signals must be repeated back by the elevator man.

Bell Code:

1. One bell to raise elevator.
2. Two bells to lower elevator.
3. Danger. Do not move elevator.

Rules for Conductors.

256 Report to and receive instructions from the Train Master and conform to the instructions issued by the Superintendent. Report to.

257 Pass the examinations required as to: Examination.

Character, habits, education and records of previous service.

Knowledge of Time-table, rules and regulations.

Characteristics of road, grades, curves, sidings, etc.

Location and indication of all fixed signals.

Construction and use of air brake appliances.

How to meet emergencies and break-downs.

Also, for color perception, strength of vision and hearing.

258 Have general charge of the train, and of all men employed on the train. Duty.

259 Be on hand, ready for duty, as directed; also, if necessary, assist in making up the train.

260 Be responsible for the movement, safety and proper care of the train, in strict accordance with the rules, special instructions and orders, and for the faithful and prompt performance of duty by the trainmen.

261 Make the safety of the train of the first importance in the discharge of your duties. Should there be any doubt as to the right of road or safety of proceeding from any cause, consult the engineman, and be equally responsible with him for the safety and proper handling of the train, and for such use of signals and other precautions as the case may require. Be vigilant Safety of train.

and cautious, not trusting alone to signals or rules for safety.

Inspection. **262** See that the train is properly made up and inspected; that it is provided with everything required by the rules, and with all spare articles and appliances to be used in emergencies; and that brake, signal whistle and steam heat tests are made before starting. Make same tests whenever any cars have been taken from (except rear) or added to the train, and before proceeding on the trip. Report all defects discovered.

Brakes. **263** All south-bound trains must be run down as far as possible to lower end of station. Hand brakes must be used by trainmen to stop trains in the station; air must not be used, except in cases of emergency.

Planks. **264** Are required to see that brakeman and porters put down planks at each car platform of trains loading on track No. 20, and that they do not take up platform planks before gates are closed.

Bulletin board. **265** Examine the bulletin board before starting upon each trip.

266 Show all train orders to your flagman as soon after receipt as practicable.

267 Push buttons have been placed on the posts at the north end of the tracks in the train shed, that are connected with indicators located in the tower. These push buttons must not be used except by conductors.

268 When a train is ready to leave the Station the conductor will notify the tower by pressing the push button. Clear signals will not be given until conductor has notified the towerman the train is ready to proceed.

269 Be careful not to signal the tower until passengers have boarded the train and everything is in readiness to proceed.

270 The push buttons are also for use of conductors of shop trains and yard switchers. When they are ready to leave the Station, they will notify the tower as outlined above.

271 Keep a memorandum of any unusual occurrence, and the details connected therewith, and be prepared to give a full report whenever required. Reports.

272 See that all reports are properly made out and promptly forwarded to the proper officer.

273 Report promptly and in writing to the Superintendent, on blanks provided for that purpose, any failure of engines, train parting, and defects discovered in roadway or bridges.

274 North-bound shop trains must be inspected before leaving the Grand Central Station, and when they are left at Mott Haven, and any damage must be reported to the Train Master.

275 South-bound shop trains must be inspected before leaving Mott Haven, and when left at the Grand Central Station, and any damage must be reported to the Train Master.

276 Make written report, on proper blanks, of all detentions to trains in your charge.

Yard conductors. **277** Yard conductors will obey promptly all orders from the Yard-master on duty.

278 Will be held responsible for the work and conduct of the men in their charge.

279 See that the men never leave a car or cars in the yard without having the brakes set on same, or wheels blocked.

280 Whenever long trains are unloading passengers on platform between Tracks No. 2 and No. 3, a train must not move on or from No. 2 track until passengers have been discharged and are out of the way of danger.

Train Baggagemen.

Report to. **281** Train Baggagemen while on trains are subject to the orders of the conductor, and to the orders of the Station Master. They are responsible for the safety of all property intrusted to their care, and will comply with the instructions of the General Baggage Agent.

Duty. **282** Report for duty in uniform at least thirty minutes before leaving time of the train; handle baggage carefully, and remain in the baggage car during the entire trip, except when called upon to perform other duties.

Examination. **283** Pass the examination required as to:

Character, habits, education and record of previous service.

Knowledge of Time-table, rules and regulations.

Characteristics of road, grades, curves, sidings, etc.

Construction and use of air brake appliances.

Also, for color perception, strength of vision, and hearing.

284 Where there is but one trainman on the train, the baggageman will have the necessary signal appliances on hand. Signal appliances.

285 Do not carry anything unless it is checked or way-billed, without permission from proper authority. Proper authority.

286 Check baggage received at stops where there are no agents, and take up checks for baggage delivered at such points. Keep all checks in possession under lock and key. Checking of baggage.

287 Before throwing off any package, be sure that it will clear the train, and that there is no person or object in the way which may be struck by it. Care in handling packages.

288 Remain in the cars at the end of the trip until all baggage and other matter is delivered and receipted for. End of trip.

289 Keep end doors of baggage cars secured, and do not allow any person to enter, except officers, mail agents, express messengers, Union News agents, and trainmen in the discharge of their duties. Not allowed in baggage car.

290 Give proper attention to the custody and delivery of United States mail, and report any irregularities promptly to the Superintendent; pay close attention to the custody and delivery of train mail. U. S. Mail.

Trainmen.

Report to. **291** Passenger Trainmen while on trains are subject to the orders of the conductor, and must obey the orders of the Station Master or Agent.

Examination. **292** Pass the examination required as to:

Character, habits, education and record of previous service.

Knowledge of time-table, rules and regulations.

Construction and use of air-brake appliances.

Also, for color perception, strength of vision and hearing.

Duty. **293** Report for duty in uniform at least thirty minutes before leaving time, and assist in making up the train when necessary.

Display signals. **294** Display prescribed signals at the rear of the train, and have all necessary supplies and signals on hand and ready for immediate use.

295 See that the water-coolers are supplied with ice and water, and know that the lamps, whistle signals, air brakes, steam heat, and all connections are in good working order.

Handle baggage. **296** Assist in handling train baggage when necessary to avoid delay.

Assist passengers. **297** Take position at the car steps to assist passengers, and, where practicable, request them to show their tickets, directing those without tickets to the office to procure them.

Flagman compare watch. **298** Compare watches with the conductor before assuming duties of flagman, and be governed by the rules of conductors, in so far as the rules pertain to your duties.

299 Look the train over carefully before starting, and know that all couplings, brake and running gear are in good order. Inspect the train as often as possible during the trip. Inspect train.

300 See that hand brakes are applied so as to avoid sliding or overheating the wheels. Braking should be changed in descending long grades. Braking.

301 In passing through sleeping, dining, or private cars, do so quietly; and if meals are being served, remove the cap. Remove cap.

302 Look to the comfort of passengers, and maintain a comfortable temperature and proper ventilation of the cars. Comfort of passengers.

303 Do not occupy seats with passengers, avoid all familiarity with them, and do not engage in conversation further than is necessary in the proper discharge of your duties. Conduct of train employes.

304 The forward trainman must have the necessary signal appliances on hand, and ready for use, and be prepared to protect the front of the train, if it is necessary to do so. Signal appliances.

305 In announcing the names of stations observe the following: Announcing stations.

On departing from a station, go to the center of the car and announce, "The next station is ....," repeating the name of the station. Just before arriving at a station, at which the train stops, announce the arrival in the same manner from inside of car, as follows: "This station is ....," the name of the station to be repeated. At meal stations the length of time the train is to stop must also be announced. Before a passenger train leaves a junction station, announce in each car the destination of the train, thus: "This train for .... The next station is ...."

If the train stops before arriving at the station platform, after the announcement has been made, the trainmen must call out, "This is not the station stop," so that passengers will not be misled, and attempt to leave the train.

Master Mechanic.

Report to. **306** The Master Mechanic will report to and receive instructions from the Assistant Manager.

Examination. **307** Will pass the examinations as to:

Character, habits, education, record of previous service, knowledge of Time-tables, rules, regulations.

Characteristics of road grades, curves.

Location and indication of all fixed signals.

Handling of a locomotive, its care and management, and economy in the use of fuel and other supplies.

Construction and use of air brakes.

Application, how to meet emergencies and breakdowns.

Color perception and strength of vision and hearing.

Duty. **308** Will have general charge of locomotive engineers, firemen, wipers and round-house men, and stationary engineers and firemen.

309 Do not permit an engineer or fireman to be assigned to service over the Harlem Line until having passed the required examinations.

310 Keep the electrical apparatus in your charge in proper order. Electrical apparatus.

311 Make frequent inspection of air compressors, and be responsible for their proper maintenance. Inspection.

312 Make frequent inspection of the locomotives, keeping them in proper repair.

313 See that cars in the yard are heated by steam satisfactorily.

314 Frequent inspection must be made of all water stations and prompt repairs made where necessary to reservoirs, pumps, tanks, pipe lines, boilers, water troughs, water columns, etc. The water stations must be constantly inspected during extreme cold weather, and kept in such condition that engines can take water at any time.

315 The inspection, repairs and renewals of all boilers will be under the Master Mechanic, who will be responsible for the care and operation of all boilers installed in heat, light, and power plants; also water supply stations, coal stations, bridges, derricks, cranes, etc. Make prompt report when any boiler shall show signs of weakness and arrange for the necessary repairs at once.

Reports condition of engines. **316** See that engineers make written report daily of work required on the engines, and see that the road foreman makes frequent inspection to know that proper work has been performed.

Records. **317** Keep an accurate tabulated record of all boilers, and see that extra parts of machinery used on the Harlem River drawbridge are ordered and received in ample time to replace any parts showing evidence of wear or need of early renewal.

Enginemen.

Report to. **318** Enginemen report to and receive their instructions from the Master Mechanic. When at the engine-house they are under the direction of the Engine Dispatcher. When on the road they are subject to the orders of the Superintendent and Train Master.

Duty. **318a** They must obey the orders of Yard masters as to shifting and making up trains, and those of conductors as to starting, stopping, and general management of trains, unless they endanger the safety of the train or require violation of rules.

319 Report for duty at the appointed time; see that the engine is in good order, furnished with necessary stores, supplies, tools and signals in good condition, and see that they are kept in the places provided for them; examine the bulletin board before starting on, and at the end of each trip compare time with the conductor before starting, regulate the speed between stations, make frequent inspection of the engine, and report failure in duty or violation of rules on the part of any employe.

320 Pass the examinations required as to: Examination.

Character, habits, education, and record of previous service.

Knowledge of Time-table, rules and regulations.

Characteristics of road, grades, curves, etc.

Location and indication of all fixed signals.

Knowledge of locomotive, its care and manage ment, and economy in use of fuel and other supplies.

Construction and use of air brake appliances.

How to meet emergencies and break-downs.

Also, for color perception, strength of vision and hearing.

321 Make the safety of the train of the first importance in the discharge of your duties. Should there be any doubt as to the right of road or safety of proceeding from any cause, consult with the conductor, and be equally responsible with him for the safety and proper handling of the train, and for such use of signals and other precautions as the case may require. Be vigilant and cautious, not trusting alone to signals or rules for safety. Safety of train first importance.

322 The engineman is jointly and equally responsible with the conductor for the safety of his train and the movement of the same in strict compliance with the rules, and he must decline to obey any orders which involve peril to his train or violation of the rules. When there is no conductor, or he is disabled, the engineman will have charge of the Responsibility.

train, and will be governed by the rules prescribed for conductors.

323 Come from round house with the fire in the engine in such condition that a heavy dense smoke will not be emitted while at the Grand Central Station. The baring of fires in and around the station is strictly prohibited.

Firing

324 Avoid creating smoke at the Grand Central Station or on the Harlem Line. **No coal must be thrown into furnace at the Grand Central Station or on the Harlem Line,** unless it should become actually necessary to replenish the fire; then only anthracite coal or coke must be thrown on, and only at such points north of the tunnel as will not be likely to bring complaints from residents. Bituminous coal must not be used under any circumstances. When fresh coal is put into fire-box, furnace door must be kept open until smoke is consumed.

Track changes.

325 When changes of track or repairs are being made in yard, run cautiously and use all care to avoid accident.

Handling of steam heat, air brake and air whistle.

326 Before leaving a terminal station apply the air brakes and steam heat when required, and allow them to remain on long enough for the inspectors or trainmen to see that the apparatus is in perfect working condition throughout the train, and when cars have been attached to or taken out, the brakes must again be applied to know that they are in working order before proceeding on the trip. In making regular stops they must be applied in such manner as to avoid discomfort to the passengers or injury to the equipment. Know that the air signal is in proper working order.

327 Always be in the cab when the engine is standing under steam, or have the fireman or other responsible employe there; the throttle must be closed, the reverse lever in center and brakes set.

328 Be particular when taking orders from the conductor that you fully understand them.

329 Show train orders to the fireman, also to the forward brakeman, and require them to read them. Train orders.

330 Do not permit any person to ride on the engine, except designated employes in the discharge of their duties, without a written order from proper authority. No one to ride on engine.

331 Personally control every movement of the engine. The fireman must not be allowed to move it, except with the approval of the proper official. Control movement.

332 Instruct the fireman in all his duties, especially as to economy in use of fuel and other supplies. Instruct fireman.

333 Must exercise care to prevent water being thrown from smokestacks when starting, and not open cylinder-cocks when using steam, nor permit overflow from injectors at station platforms. Handling of engine.

334 Start carefully on receiving proper signal, avoid slipping driving wheels, observe markers, or have fireman do so, to know that train is complete.

335 Engine bell must not be rung except where necessary to warn persons walking on the tracks between 110th and 134th Streets. Ringing engine bell.

Signal appliances.

336 Keep a lighted red lantern, with three torpedoes attached, in cab of engine, where it cannot be seen by passing trains, for use in case of necessity.

337 Engine decks must not be swept or washed off while engine is in the train shed. Care must be used so that refuse oil and coal will not be thrown on the platforms.

Sand.

Do not sand the rail while passing over switches or interlocking connections.

Air brake test.

338 Test the air brake one half mile from stations where engines have been changed, or where cars have been taken on or left; also, at least one mile before reaching railroad crossings, drawbridges, and at other hazardous places, and before going down heavy grades, and in case the brakes do not hold, must at once signal for brakes. Such test to be made by applying the brakes with sufficient force to ascertain whether they are working properly.

Steam should not be shut off when making the test, if the conditions are such as do not require it.

Crossing bridges.

339 Brakes must not be applied or released while crossing bridges or trestles except in cases of emergency.

Dampers.

340 Keep the dampers of ash-pans closed while crossing bridges or trestles. Do not permit ash-pans to be cleaned while passing over switches or frogs, in front of stations, or on crossings. As far as practicable, they should be cleaned at the designated points only. See that ashes are wet down and that they are leveled to the height of the rail.

341 Report by telegraph all switch or other signals not properly lighted or displayed. Improper signals.

342 Call aloud to the fireman the indications of all fixed signals as they come into view, and know the fireman repeats the same information. Call signals.

343 When signals are obscured by fog or otherwise, bring your train under immediate control and run cautiously until you can positively see and distinguish the signals. Do not at any time run at any speed at which your train cannot be brought to a full stop from a point at which the home signals can be plainly seen, and before reaching the same; but if for any reason any part of the train passes the home signal while same is at danger, the train must back within the block by hand signal from the towerman, and not proceed until signal has cleared in the usual way, or until Clearance Card has been received from the towerman, except as provided in Rule No. 345, making full report to the Superintendent in writing of each occurrence. Obscured signals.

344 Be particular, when stopping at home signals, on the Harlem Line, not to let the leading wheels pass beyond the signal. The electric circuit for the next block in advance commences at the home signal, and any wheels standing thereon block the section. Engines blocking section.

345 Never pass a home signal when set at danger, or when it cannot be plainly seen to indicate safety, except that when fixed signals from any cause cannot be used, enginemen will take green hand signals from operators in the Block signal tower, and proceed to Clearance cards.

tower and there get **clearance card,** except at second section on No. 3 and 4 tracks at Harlem River drawbridge, where green hand signal will be given by bridgeman, and on No. 3 and 4 tracks at 96th Street, where green hand signal will be given by towerman, and proceed with caution to next fixed signal.

Engine on main line.

346 Never allow engine to stand on main line unless properly protected under the rules.

347 Enginemen will be held directly responsible in event of the engine in their charge colliding with a preceding train within the yard limits.

Care in use of property.

348 Be careful in the use of all property of the company. Never allow tank spouts, water cranes, hose pipes, or coal chutes to be moved to or from the tender while engine is in motion; also see that the spouts are empty before being moved, and that they are replaced in proper position and secured before leaving them.

Safety valves.

349 Never interfere with the safety valves, or allow the boiler pressure to be above the limit at which the valves are set.

Look back frequently.

350 When running freight trains, look back frequently to see that no portion of the train has become detached or derailed.

Double-headers.

351 When a train has more than one engine the requirements of the rules apply alike to the engineman of each engine, except that the use of the engine bell and whistle shall be limited to the leading engine.

352 At the end of each trip report any work required before engine is again assigned to service.

353 Report to the Master Mechanic any defect in or improper condition of engine. If engine is disabled on the road, make immediate report by telegraph to the Superintendent.

354 Report immediately to the Superintendent all accidents, injury to persons or property, and unusual detention of trains, using the forms provided for that purpose. Fill the blanks out properly, and give accurately and concisely all essential details. Reports.

Firemen.

355 Pass the examinations required as to: Examination.

Character, habits, education, and record of previous service.

Knowledge of Time-table, rules and regulations.

Location and indication of all fixed signals.

Knowledge of economy in use of fuel and other supplies.

Construction and use of air brake appliances.

Also, for color perception, strength of vision and hearing.

356 Report for duty at the required time, and assist in switching and making up train when necessary. Duty.

357 Obey the orders of the engineman respecting the proper use of fuel and the manner of performing their work.

358 Be familiar with the train rules that apply to the protection of trains, understand the use of all signals, and be prepared to use them promptly when required, as provided in the rules.

Examine bulletin board.

359 Examine the bulletin board before starting on each trip, and be familiar with all special orders pertaining to their trains or engines. Keep a constant lookout ahead when not engaged in firing, and give instant notice to the engineman of any danger signals or obstructions on the track.

Take charge of engine.

360 Take charge of the engine in the absence of the engineman, and do not leave it until his return, nor permit any unauthorized person to be upon it.

Engineman disabled.

361 In case the engineman becomes disabled, stop the engine and report to the conductor.

Not to run engine.

362 Do not run an engine in the absence of the engineman without instructions from the Superintendent, unless in some emergency you are instructed to do so by the conductor or some officer in authority.

Firing.

363 Avoid firing so as to cause the emission of black smoke at any time.

Call signals.

364 Carefully notice the position and indication of all fixed signals, and call them aloud to the engineman, and know that he repeats the same information. Keep in mind all orders and notices regarding the movement of trains, so as to be prepared to correct any oversight or mistake if there should be any occasion for so doing.

Rules for Engineer Maintenance of Way.

365 The maintenance of way and structures is in charge of the Engineer Maintenance of Way, reporting to the Manager on the various matters under his jurisdiction. Will be assisted by a Supervisor of Track, and a Supervisor of Signals. Organization.

366 Will be responsible to the Manager for the safe, efficient and economical construction and maintenance of all of the work under his charge. Responsibility.

367 Work in close harmony with the Superintendent. Superintendent.

368 Be thoroughly conversant with all special circulars issued from the general office for his guidance, and promptly communicate to his subordinates all general instructions issued by the manager. Circulars

Supervisor of Track

369 Reports to the Engineer Maintenance of Way, and is responsible for the safe condition and proper maintenance of all tunnels, bridges, trestles, culverts, retaining-walls, turn-tables, buildings, platforms, track-scales, coaling stations, road-bed, main and side-tracks, sea-walls, and any other structures affecting the tracks. General duties.

See that proper slopes and ditches are preserved; that culverts and drains are kept open, that everything liable to obstruct any track is removed, and take all necessary measures to prevent accident or delay to trains.

370 He will be assisted by the necessary foremen, laborers, extra gangs, wrecking gangs, watchmen, masons, carpenters, tinsmiths, painters, bridgemen, drawbridge operators, and such additional forces as may be assigned to him for special work. He will see that equipment under his charge is always ready for service.

371 See that all track repairs are performed systematically, starting on one end of each section and working continuously towards the other so that each day's work will show definite progress.

372 Be conversant with standard plans, specifications and rules.

373 Acquaint yourself fully with the use of signals, see that they are understood by your subordinates, and see that proper stop and slow signals are displayed when construction or repair work is being done.

374 See that economy is exercised in the use of labor, tools, and material. Employ such workmen as may be necessary, subject to the approval of your superior officer, and see that all employees are provided with the necessary tools, that they have under them assistants and laborers who are punctual and faithful in the discharge of their duties, and that their force is organized so as to give the most effective service. See that the actual time worked, occupations, and rates of the men are correctly stated on the pay rolls, and that no tools or material are sold or loaned unless authorized in writing by the Engineer Maintenance of Way. See that all materials are correct as represented on bills, and suitable for the purposes required, and that bills are checked and promptly returned to the proper officer. In case material is not in accordance with specifications, make report, showing discrepancies and hold until instructions are received. See that every employee who is relieved, properly accounts for or returns all passes, keys, blanks, badges, tools or material which have been in his charge. See that all work under your charge is performed in a neat and substantial manner.

375 During the last three months of each year make a personal examination of every structure under your charge, and make reports on the proper blanks to be transmitted to the Engineer Maintenance of Way not later than December 31st of each year. Annual inspection.

376 On the last day of each of the remaining three quarters of the year, reports based upon an examination of each structure shall be rendered to the Engineer Maintenance of Way, noting any modification of the aforesaid annual report. Quarterly inspection.

377 See that the following items are given particular attention during the inspection of all structures under your charge. Details of inspections.

378 In cases requiring urgent attention, report the facts to the Engineer Maintenance of Way, and take immediate precautions to prevent accident. Urgent repairs.

379 Examine each retaining-wall, culvert, pier, and abutment or other masonry structures, to discover Masonry foundation.

undermining, scouring, bulging, cracking, settlement or other indication of failure.

Bridge-seats. **380** See that bridge-seats are level, firmly bedded and free from cracks or evidence of crushing. See that bridge-seats and roller nests are kept clean and free from rubbish and cinders.

Bed-plates. **381** Bed-plates should be level, and in proper position, and have uniform bearing.

Rollers. **382** Rollers should move freely, with their axes at right angles to the line of the bridge.

Sole-plates and pedestals. **383** Sole-plates and pedestals should be free from flaws and cracks, and should be firmly attached to the main members.

Posts. **384** Posts of viaducts and those supporting girders or trusses should be free from bends or bulges, and all joints should bear firmly and closely against each other.

Main trusses. **385** Main trusses should have the tension-members (eye-bars, rods and bottom chords), free from slackness and in perfect adjustment, so that they will be equally strained per square inch in any one panel. Compression members (top-chords and posts) should be straight, free from bulges or bends, with joints bearing firmly and closely against each other. Counter-rods should never be loose nor very tight, but should be adjusted while there is no load on the bridge, so that they will be taut, and no more.

Girders. **386** Girders should be stiff, free from undue deflection or lateral motion.

387 Lateral system (sway-bracing and lateral-bracing) of trusses, girders and viaducts should be in proper adjustment, tight and not overstrained. Lateral system.

388 Solid trough and rail floors should be examined with a view to the discovery of corrosion. Trough and rail floors.

389 Shelf-angles supporting ties on through plate girders should be closely examined for loose, missing or defective rivets, and especial attention should be given to the condition of the ends of the wooden ties bearing on the angles. Shelf-angles.

390 Floor-beams and stringers should be closely and frequently examined for any cracking of connection angles, the presence of loose, defective or missing rivets or for shearing and crushing of webs and flanges at all points of connection with each other, and where the floor-beams connect with hangers or posts. Floor-beam and stringer connections.

391 Floor-beams and stringers, and the top-chords of trusses that support directly the tie-floor should be free from undue deflection or lateral motion. Floor-beams and stringers, etc.

392 Pins should be carefully inspected for evidence of bending, wear or **loose nuts**. Pins.

393 Rivets in all connections should be tapped with a hammer at least once a year to detect loose rivets, and any that cannot be tightened at once should be spotted with white paint, and their numbers and location reported. Any missing rivets should be replaced and reported at once. Rivets.

394 Hangers supporting floor-beams require the closest attention. Where they consist of round or Hangers.

square iron their bearing around the pins should always be equal and uniform over half the circumference of the latter, and they should be critically inspected at the semi-circle for flaws or fractures. The nuts on the ends of hangers should never be loose, and should have jamb-nuts to prevent their movement under the jar of trains. Plate hangers should be closely examined for loose rivets, and for any indication of cracking or shearing.

Castings. **395** Castings should be frequently examined with great care for the discovery of cracks, breaks or flaws, and any such discovered should at once be reported. Particular attention should be given to cast connections at junction of posts with top and bottom chords of trusses.

Drainage. **396** Drain-holes should be drilled in any member that permits the collection of water, and all existing drain-holes should be frequently cleaned.

Painting. **397** All iron bridges should be thoroughly covered with paint so as to prevent corrosion. No paint shall be applied on outside surfaces in wet or freezing weather, nor shall any surfaces be painted until they are cleaned and dried, or until the previous coating is thoroughly dry. Surfaces covered with rust, grease, dirt or other foreign substances shall be thoroughly cleaned by wire brushes, scraping or other suitable method. On old iron work, if the original paint is in fair condition, one coat of Formula "F" will suffice, after first touching up spots; but when the paint is in poor condition, thoroughly clean the structure and apply a priming coat of Formula "E" (Pure Red Lead and Linseed Oil) and two coats of Formula "F" (N. Y. C. Asphaltum Varnish). The dates of erection and painting of bridges shall be plainly indicated on all structures.

398 All bents of trestles should stand perfectly plumb, and should be free from settlement or lateral motion under traffic. The foundations under trestles should be frequently examined for evidence of undermining or scouring. All sills resting on blocking shall be kept free from dirt. **Bents.**

399 Provide barrels, with floating lids and buckets, constantly filled with water, at each end of all wooden bridges and short trestles, and at suitable intervals on long trestles. **Barrels, water.**

400 Ties and guard-timbers on all bridges should be maintained in sound condition, and any missing floor bolts should immediately be replaced. **Ties and guard-timbers.**

401 The rails of the main track on bridges should be spiked at every other tie. Spikes must not be driven in angle bar slots on bridges. **Spiking.**

402 On all bridges exceeding 20 feet in clear span there should be an inside rail guard, as shown on standard plans. **Guard rail.**

403 During the inspection of bridges and trestles, pay particular attention to the action of the structures, or a part thereof, under passing trains. Excessive deflection, swaying, twisting, or rattling of parts is sure evidence that attention is needed, and the facts should **General action.**

be reported at once. Unusual deflections should be instrumentally measured.

Corrosion. **404** All overhead bridges subject to the destructive influence of locomotive gases should be frequently examined, and all parts badly deteriorated should be immediately reported for the necessary strengthening or replacing.

Defective members. **405** Look carefully for any members of any part of any structure that may be defective, and any other items not herein specified affecting the safety of the structures.

Use of labor. **406** Use ordinary labor wherever possible for handling material, excavating for foundations, scrapping bridges, concreting, etc.

Foundations, new work. **407** See that no structure is started until the foundations have been, by him personally, carefully examined and approved. The bottom of all footing-courses shall extend below frost line, and shall be of sufficient depth to insure an unyielding and solid foundation, thoroughly protected from all danger of scour and undermining, and where necessary piling shall be used.

Excavations. **408** Excavations shall be made as carefully as possible with the use of any necessary shoring or sheet-piling, so as to least affect the neighboring structures or track, and so as not to cause any danger of slides.

Drawbridge inspection and maintenance. **409** Make a personal examination of the Harlem River Drawbridge at least every 30 days, and examine the bridge while in operation to see that all parts, such as wedges, latches, lifts, gearing, etc., are working properly and are being well and efficiently maintained.

410 See that the operators in charge of the bridges are properly qualified for their work and understand the operation of the various parts of the machinery.

Where bridges are operated both day and night, it should be distinctly understood by all concerned that the day operator is in charge of the bridge, and will be held responsible for proper daily maintenance and reports of defects or breakages.

411 See that the machinery and engine houses are maintained in a neat and clean condition, that all waste is kept in a can provided for the purpose, and that there is no grease, oil or dirt accumulation which may cause fire or deteriorate the structure.

412 Carefully watch all portions of structures hidden from view and not convenient for ready inspection, such as under-supports of platforms and buildings, truss-rods and other members subject to corrosive action of locomotive gases, engine house smoke-jacks, roof cornices, water-tank hoops, etc. Frequently examine platforms used by passengers or employees and repair quickly any defects that might cause injury. See that shop roof trusses are not overloaded with shafting. Hidden defects.

413 All buildings shall be neatly painted and properly maintained, especially those used by the public. Small defects, such as broken glass, broken Maintenance of buildings.

locks, broken bolts, broken woodwork, etc., shall receive quick attention so as not to invite criticism. Water closet facilities shall be maintained in good order so that the Agent will have no excuse for not keeping them neat and clean.

Station platforms. **414** Platforms to all stations shall be inclosed beneath by vertical slats to prevent the deposit of scrap iron, paper, rubbish, etc.

Coal boxes. **415** Unsightly coal boxes around signal towers and stations are especially undesirable and, where necessary, should be placed in the rear of buildings out of view.

Time to paint. **416** All exterior painting must be started as early as possible in the Spring for completion before the beginning of Summer travel. During the Winter months attention can be given to the interiors of stations. No paint shall be applied to outside surfaces in wet or freezing weather, nor shall any surfaces be painted until they are cleaned and dried, or until the previous coating is thoroughly dried.

Filling pores. **417** Should woodwork be old and very dry and porous, first apply a coat of pure linseed-oil to fill the pores and prevent chalking.

Kind of depôt paint. **418** For buildings Formula "C" will be used for the body color, and Formula "D" for the trimming color, except that where shingles are used Green Stain will be substituted for the paint. One coat will usually be sufficient for re-painting buildings, but where necessary two coats or more will be used. Three coats shall be used for all new work.

419 Buildings in the Motive Power Department subjected to the constant effect of locomotive gases and smoke shall be painted lead color, Formula "Q." The interior of Motive Power buildings not used for office purposes shall be whitewashed at least once a year, and oftener if necessary for keeping the interior fresh, neat and clean. Smoke-jacks shall be properly maintained and broken lights of glass shall be promptly replaced. **Buildings in Motive Power Department.**

420 Before buildings are repainted all minor repairs shall be made. **Minor repairs.**

421 The dates of erection and painting of all buildings, including the designation of the paint used, shall be plainly indicated on the structures. **Dates, painting.**

422 See that all signs are neatly painted as directed by the Engineer Maintenance of Way. **Signs.**

423 Monthly examinations and tests shall be made of all track-scales. **Scales.**

424 Frequent examinations shall be made of all water stations, and prompt repairs shall be made where necessary to tanks, water columns, etc. **Water station examinations.**

425 The following rules shall be observed in the location and construction of buildings and platforms: **Buildings and platforms, location and construction.**

425-a Except in the case of special concrete platforms the tops of all low platforms adjacent to main track shall not be higher than the top of the rail.

425-b The top of all special concrete or wooden platforms, at stations where that style of construction is approved by the Engineer Maintenance of Way, shall be 12 inches above the base of the rail, with the edge thereof 5 feet 3 inches from and parallel to the center line of the track.

425-c The tops of all freight platforms on side tracks, for general use, should be four feet above the top of the rail on the side track (conforming to the grade of the track) and the edge of the platform 5 feet 6 inches from the center of the track.

425-d No building shall be located nearer than seven feet six inches in the clear from the center of the main track, nor nearer than seven feet in the clear from the center of any side-track.

425-e Buildings, wherever practicable, should be located on the outside of curves, and far enough from road crossings to avoid obstructing the view either of trainmen or travelers on the highway or street.

Buildings belonging to outsiders.

426 See that structures belonging to outsiders, located upon the property of the Railroad Company, are maintained in a neat and safe manner, and painted so that they will at all times present a good appearance.

Report of fire losses.

427 Carefully observe, for insurance purposes, instructions regarding reports of fire losses and proper valuations on structures.

Tunnel inspection.

428 Personally examine at least once a month Park Avenue Tunnel. A tunnel inspection car shall be run through this tunnel once a month for the purpose of making careful sledge and bar tests to detect loose and fragmentary portions of roof and sides. See that neighboring owners do not commit acts endangering the safety of the Railroad, and that particular care is taken by trackmen to keep signal pipe, wires, and other signal apparatus free from all obstructions.

429 Personally see that all section foremen and other foremen are thoroughly acquainted with all special circulars and instructions, and with the rules herein contained applicable to their duties. Rules.

430 See that all signs and switch-targets are maintained in proper condition, and are freshly painted twice each year, viz., April 1st and October 1st. Signs and targets.

431 Particular attention will be paid to the policing and cleanliness of the right-of-way and property of the company. Policing.

432 In cases of accidents or wrecks or other detentions of trains, you will go promptly to the spot, taking all necessary tools and a force of laborers sufficient for the emergency, and do all in your power to clear the track and facilitate the movement of trains. Promptly send a telegraphic report to the Manager and Engineer Maintenance of Way, stating briefly the cause and extent of damage and detention of trains. Wrecks.

433 See that the wrecking equipment is at all times in accordance with standard requirements, in first-class condition, and always ready for use. Also have your wrecking force so organized that it will be ready to leave headquarters not later than 40 minutes after the receipt of notice from the operator. Promptly and thoroughly clean up all debris from the wreck so that the public will not receive impressions that wrecks are common occurrences. Wrecking equipment.

Maintenance of way equipment and time of wrecking.

434 Maintenance of way equipment, including wrecking equipment, shall be maintained in proper condition, ready at all times for emergencies. The heavy running equipment should be frequently tested to see that the journals are in good shape, so that they will not run hot. The steam crane should at all times be equipped with the necessary fuel and appliances for service on short notice.

Snow storms and wash-outs.

435 Be fully prepared for handling snow storms and washouts, and will observe the following instructions:

435-a Every man in the employ of the Maintenance of Way Department should have a duty assigned to him in connection with fighting snow, and he shall know what will be expected in severe storms.

435-b Keep in touch with the Train Dispatchers to learn the conditions at various points on the division, so that at the first sign of trouble forces will be organized.

435-c Prepare to fight snow upon the first sign of trouble.

435-d Detail sufficient men during the night and day to pay particular attention to switches during snow storms, as this is the place where trouble is first experienced.

435-e During long continued storms men will be worked in relays, so that one gang can be resting while the other is working.

435-f Make ample arrangements for feeding the men with coffee and sandwiches during bad storms, so that they can work to their full efficiency.

435-g Increase the force for fighting snow on advice from the Engineer Maintenance of Way, except in cases of emergency, when you can use your own judgment without waiting for advice. Such course, however, is to be promptly reported.

435-h The regular rates of wages will always be paid for this class of service, unless additional rates are advisable to obtain men, in which case the facts should be reported to the Engineer Maintenance of Way.

436 Earnestly endeavor to improve the line and surface of all tracks, especially main tracks, and see that every measure is taken to insure their smooth riding qualities and safety. Line and surface.

437 The track on bridges and approaches must always be kept in good line and surface. Track on bridges.

438 Personally see that no ties are removed from the track that are good for one year's additional service. Ties good for one year.

439 Personally examine ties in track prior to October 1st each year, and prepare the annual statement of quantities required for ensuing season. Tie renewals.

440 See that all bridge-seats are maintained free from all dirt and debris, and that the approaches to all bridges are in proper condition. Bridge-seats.

441 See that no obstructions are maintained on either side of the main track within seven feet six inches from the center thereof, that ties, lumber and other material are not piled within eight feet of the Side obstructions.

nearest rail, and that all material taken out of bridges is gathered and neatly piled at a distance.

Contractors. **442** Keep watch over all work done by contractors or others on his division, and see that they do not obstruct the track or bridges to the danger of passing trains.

Station-grounds. **443** See that snow is promptly removed from the tracks and from around station-grounds and other buildings used by the public.

Highways. **444** See that particular attention is paid to the clearing of obstructions in the neighborhood of highway crossings that would obscure from the public a clear view of approaching trains.

Bridge warnings. Overhead wires. **445** See that the Section Foremen keep bridge warnings in a proper state of repair and at the proper height, and that overhead wires are preserved at sufficient heights—at least twenty-five (25) feet above top of rail—to prevent accident to trainmen.

Material. **446** Use proper judgment in ordering only such materials as are best suited for the purpose for which they are to be used, and in the proper quantities for prompt consumption.

Inspection. **447** Walk over a portion of the division daily, and pass over all of it on foot at least once a month. Spend most of the time on the road, and see that the section foremen and their men fully understand and perform their duties.

Alignment and elevation. **448** Personally observe the alignment and elevation of curves, and instruct section foremen about the proper elevation for every curve on the division.

449 Frequently examine track-gauges and levels and see that they are in accordance with the standard furnished by the Engineer Maintenance of Way. Track levels and gauges.

450 Closely watch all rolling-stock on the division and promptly report any locomotives or cars whose tires are worn over one-fourth inch in depth, or that have flat wheels. Worn tires and flat wheels.

451 Long stringers and other emergency material shall always be kept easily available at headquarters for prompt use in case of washouts or other accidents. Emergency material.

452 See that no encroachments are made on the property of the Railroad Company, except when properly authorized by lease or agreement, and prevent any railroad, telegraph, telephone, or power transmission line from crossing, at grade, under or over the tracks of this Company, without due authority. Encroachments.

453 New yards and new side-tracks shall not be turned over to the use of the Operating Department until they are ballasted and ready for permanent use. Yard and side-tracks.

Section, Work Train and Extra Gang Foremen.

454 Section, work train and extra gang foremen will report to and receive their orders from the Supervisor of Track, and under his direction will have charge of the labor necessary for the maintenance of the roadbed and track. General duties.

455 Will be assisted by the necessary section laborers, watchmen and such additional forces as may be assigned to them for special work. Engage personally in your work, except where large gangs are employed, when your entire time may be required for supervision.

Examination. **456** Pass examination required as to:
Character, habits and record of previous service.
Knowledge of Time-table, rules and regulations.
Also for color perception, strength of vision and hearing.

457 Upon the approach of a train move out of the way promptly, removing tools to a safe distance from the track. Take special care, under all conditions, to guard against personal injury to employees.

Drainage. **458** Good drainage is most essential, and the farther water is removed from the track and the sooner it can be diverted from the roadbed the more stable will become the track.

Ditches. **459** All ditches should, at all times, be in good condition, and they must be in accordance with standard plan. They should be generally parallel with the track, except at inlets and outlets, where they should diverge from the roadbed so as not to injure the embankments. They must be of the necessary size to pass all water freely during the heaviest rains.

Dirt on sides of cuts. **460** All earth from ditches or elsewhere must be deposited over the sides of adjacent embankments, immediately leveled off, and **under no circumstances shall it be thrown on the sides of cuts.**

461 Ditches in cuts should always be below the bottom of the old ballast. Ditches deep enough.

462 During heavy wind and rain storms, abrupt changes in temperature, when there is an excessive number of broken rails, or where some special operating service is to be performed, day or night, great precaution must be taken to prevent accidents. Section Foremen must be out with a sufficient force of men, all supplied with proper signals, tools and instructions, to insure the safety of trains. Storms and track walking.

463 When possible, grade-stakes for the elevation of the top of the rail and for alignment will be given by the Supervisor of Track. Grade-stakes.

464 Trackmen must under no circumstances raise the surface of the track in tunnels or under overhead structures unless under special orders from the Supervisor of Track; nor shall they raise the grade by blocking up under iron bridges without special instructions from the Engineer Maintenance of Way, to be transmitted through the Supervisor. Tracks under bridges and tunnels.

465 Ties shall be located as shown in the plan of standard track. Eighteen ties per 30-foot rail and 20 ties per 33-foot rail will be used in main passenger tracks; 16 ties per 30-foot rail and 18 ties per 33-foot rail will be used on other main tracks. Running side-tracks will be laid with 16 ties per 30-foot rail, and storage tracks with 14 ties per 30-foot rail. Number of ties.

Renewal of ties.

466 Care shall be taken to avoid renewing ties to a face. Except in special instances the maximum should be about three ties per rail length, and when this number is exceeded the Supervisor will personally look into the case to see that judgment has been used. The average number of tie renewals per year should not exceed two ties per rail length, and some of the lines will not require more than an average of one tie per rail length.

Joint ties.

467 The largest and best ties will be selected for the joints. All ties will be laid at right angles to the tracks, and none shall be placed obliquely to suit irregular joints.

Ends of ties.

468 The ends of all cross-ties will be laid to a line on the south and west sides of the track. On double tracks the ties will be lined on the outside of both tracks, regardless of curves.

Length ties.

469 All new ties furnished should not vary more than one inch from eight feet in length; any furnished less than seven feet eleven inches long should be rejected; and any exceeding eight feet one inch long should be sawed off to the proper length. In such cases the Supervisor of Track should be given a list of the ties that do not conform with the specifications.

Handling and laying ties.

470 Cross-ties shall not be damaged by sticking picks in them, or by using hammers in spacing, and should never be notched, but, if necessary, may be adzed to obtain a true and uniform bearing for the base of rail. Heart side of ties should always be turned down.

471 Tie-plugs should always be kept on hand and taken out each day with the gang. The invariable rule must be to plug every hole wherever a spike is drawn. Tie plugs.

472 When track heaves the ties shall not be adzed, but shims shall be used to bring the track to proper surface. For shims more than one inch in thickness holes must be bored in them, and spikes of extra length and braces shall be used. Shims.

473 Remove shims from track as early as possible in the spring, and always before surfacing or ballasting. Removal of shims.

474 All ties removed from the track must be gathered up at the close of each day and placed in a safe and convenient place for loading on cars. Old ties will be separated into two classes, (1) those fit for use in sidings, and (2) those unfit for one year's additional service—to be burned or otherwise disposed of. No ties shall be condemned as unfit for further use until they have been examined by the Supervisor of Track. Old ties removed from the track unfit for one year's additional service will be given to the section foremen and sectionmen for firewood purposes, free of charge, not to exceed 200 per annum for each employe. The remaining old ties will either be sold by the Railroad Company or burned. Old ties.

475 New ties must not be scattered along the road, but if not ready for immediate use shall be stacked in piles of fifty each according to standard plan. Piling new ties.

476 All rail for laying in main line tracks, whether new or second-hand, shall not be thrown off Unloading rail.

of the cars roughly, but shall be unloaded with a derrick or other special method approved by the Engineer Maintenance of Way to prevent injury. All new rails must be unloaded in the same consecutive order as the rolling mill invoices and laid with brand on outside of track.

Laying rails. **477** All rails must be laid in accordance with the standard plan; the joints must be "broken," care being taken to have them within two inches of the center of the opposite rail; all joints and fastenings must have the full number of bolts; nuts must be screwed up tight with the nut on the inside, except on rails of seventy pounds per yard or less, when they shall be placed on the outside. Switch points for making temporary connections between old and new rail shall always be of the same section as the higher rail, to prevent the false flange on worn tires from causing spread track.

Second-class rails. **478** Second-class rail shall be reserved for use in switch leads or yards.

Loosening bolts. **479** In order to prevent undue stresses in rails due to contraction in winter and expansion in summer, all nuts shall be loosened and then retightened during a warm day in the spring and during a cold day in the fall. This action permits the rail to adjust itself to the season's temperature. At all other times the bolts must be kept tight.

480 During hot weather tracks shall be carefully watched to detect any tendency of the rails to expand and throw the track out of line. Only a minimum amount of track should be left empty at any time, and when in this condition the bolts should be slack.

481 Rails shall be spiked on the inside and outside of each tie, care being taken that the spikes are driven perpendicularly, and that they do not lean inward nor outward. Spikes must be driven not less than two inches from the edge of the tie, and the outside spikes must be opposite each other, and the inside spikes must be opposite each other.

482 Spikes must not be driven in angle-bar slots on bridges.

483 When it is necessary to make bolt-holes in the rails a drill must be used.

484 Rails less than fourteen feet in length will not be allowed in the main track, and when it is necessary to use short lengths they will be placed on tangents or on the inside of curves.

485 Important rail renewals will be done under the direct supervision of the Supervisor of Track.

486 Special lengths of rails will be furnished for adjusting lengths of curves so as to prevent joints from running ahead of their proper positions.

487 Rails on curves of three degrees and over shall be curved in accordance wlth the following table:

Middle Ordinates in Inches for Curving Rails.

Degrees of Curves.	CHORD LENGTHS IN FEET.												
	100	**50**	**33**	**30**	**28**	**26**	**24**	**22**	**20**	**18**	**16**	**14**	**12**
1°	2½	⅝	5/16	¼	3/16	3/16	⅛	⅛	⅛	1/16	1/16	1/16	1/16
2	5¼	1¼	9/16	½	7/16	⅜	5/16	¼	¼	3/16	⅛	⅛	1/16
3	8	2	⅞	11/16	⅝	9/16	7/16	⅜	5/16	¼	¼	3/16	⅛
4	10½	2⅝	1⅛	15/16	⅞	¾	⅝	½	½	⅜	5/16	¼	3/16
5	13	3¼	1 7/16	1 3/16	1 1/16	⅞	¾	⅝	9/16	7/16	⅜	¼	3/16
6	15¾	4	1 11/16	1 7/16	1¼	1 1/16	15/16	13/16	⅝	½	7/16	5/16	¼
7	18¼	4⅝	2	1 11/16	1½	1¼	1 1/16	⅞	¾	⅝	½	⅜	¼
8	21	5¼	2¼	1 15/16	1 11/16	1 7/16	1 3/16	1 1/16	⅞	11/16	9/16	½	5/16
9	23½	5⅞	2 9/16	2⅛	1⅞	1⅝	1⅜	1⅛	15/16	¾	⅝	½	⅜
10	26¼	6½	2⅞	2⅜	2 1/16	1 13/16	1½	1 5/16	1 1/16	⅞	11/16	9/16	⅜
11	29	7¼	3⅛	2⅝	2¼	2	1 11/16	1 7/16	1 3/16	15/16	¾	⅝	7/16
12	31½	7⅞	3 7/16	2⅞	2½	2 3/16	1 13/16	1 9/16	1¼	1 1/16	⅞	⅝	½
13	34	8½	3 11/16	3 1/16	2 11/16	2 5/16	2	1 11/16	1⅜	1⅛	15/16	11/16	½
14	36¾	9¼	4	3 5/16	2⅞	2½	2⅛	1 13/16	1½	1 3/16	1	¾	9/16
15	39¼	9⅞	4 5/16	3 9/16	3⅛	2 11/16	2¼	1 15/16	1 9/16	1 5/16	1 1/16	13/16	⅝
16	42	10½	4 9/16	3¾	3 5/16	2⅞	2 7/16	2 1/16	1 11/16	1⅜	1⅛	⅞	⅝
17	44½	11⅛	4 13/16	4	3½	3 1/16	2 9/16	2 3/16	1 13/16	1 7/16	1 3/16	⅞	11/16
18	47¼	11⅞	5⅛	4¼	3 11/16	3 3/16	2 11/16	2 5/16	1⅞	1 9/16	1¼	15/16	11/16
19	49¾	12½	5⅜	4½	3⅞	3⅜	2⅞	2 7/16	2	1⅝	1 5/16	1	¾
20	52½	13⅛	5 11/16	4¾	4⅛	3 9/16	3	2 9/16	2⅛	1 11/16	1⅜	1 1/16	13/16
21			6	4 15/16	4 5/16	3¾	3 3/16	2 11/16	2 3/16	1 13/16	1 7/16	1⅛	⅞
22			6¼	5 3/16	4½	3 15/16	3 5/16	2 13/16	2 5/16	1⅞	1½	1 3/16	⅞
23			6½	5 7/16	4 11/16	4 1/16	3 7/16	2 15/16	2⅜	1 15/16	1 9/16	1 3/16	15/16
24			6 13/16	5⅝	4 15/16	4¼	3⅝	3 1/16	2½	2 1/16	1 11/16	1¼	15/16
25			7 1/16	5⅞	5⅛	4 7/16	3¾	3 3/16	2⅝	2⅛	1¾	1 5/16	1
26			7⅜	6 1/16	5 5/16	4⅝	3⅞	3 5/16	2 11/16	2 3/16	1 13/16	1⅜	1
27			7⅝	6 5/16	5½	4¾	4 1/16	3 7/16	2 13/16	2 5/16	1⅞	1 7/16	1 1/16
28			7 15/16	6 9/16	5 11/16	4 15/16	4 3/16	3 9/16	2 15/16	2⅜	1 15/16	1 7/16	1⅛
29			8 3/16	6 13/16	5⅞	5⅛	4⅜	3⅝	3	2 7/16	2	1½	1⅛

(Ordinates at the quarters are ¾ of Middle-Ordinates.)

488 Iron shims for separating joints must always be used for laying track; wooden shims will not answer, and must not be used. The proper thickness of shims for thirty and thirty-three feet rails are as follows: **Expansion at joints.**

At 100	degrees	Fahr.	temperature,	1/16	in.
" 80	"	"	"	1/8	"
" 60	"	"	"	3/16	"
" 40	"	"	"	1/4	"
" 20	"	"	"	5/16	"
Zero	"	"	"	3/8	"

When the temperature falls below zero Fahr. no rails shall be laid without instructions from the Engineer Maintenance of Way. Each foreman laying new rail shall provide himself with a thermometer.

489 Rails adjoining others of a different height must have a step-chair to bring the tops of the rails to the same level, and they shall be connected with compromise splices. **Step-chairs or compromise splices.**

490 In taking up rails which are to be relaid in main tracks, the following instructions should be strictly observed so that the rails may be relaid in the same order in which they were removed. **Relaying rails.**

490-a The cars on which the rails are loaded should be marked A, B, C, etc., until the alphabet is exhausted, then AA, AB, AC, etc., then BA, BC, BD, etc.

490-b The rails as loaded should be marked with paint on the **West** end of each rail as follows: the South rail even numbers, 2, 4, 6, 8, 10, 12, 14, etc.

The North rail odd numbers, 1, 3, 5, 7, 9, 11, 13, etc. The numbers may be repeated for each car.

490-c Each car should have a card securely fastened thereon, giving its alphabetical designation, and the number of rails contained. For instance, N. Y. C. 15732,

A-40 rails odd,
A-40 " even.

490-d Care should be taken to forward the cars in their correct order so as to reduce the switching at the point of destination.

490-e A notice should be sent to consignee each day giving car numbers, designations (A, B, etc.) and the number of rails—odd or even—on each car.

490-f The consignee will sort the cars, unload and lay the rail in exactly the same order as taken up.

Braces on curves.

491 Curves of three degrees or over must be braced on both inside and outside rails, unless tie-plates are used. Braces must be placed opposite each other on the same tie. Curves of from three to six degrees must have four braces to each 30-foot rail. Curves of six degrees and over shall have six braces to each 30-foot rail.

Tie-plates.

492 Tie-plates on new ties shall be driven home with the aid of a special steel plate and sledge before the ties are placed in the track, care being taken to locate the tie-plates so that the track will be spiked to correct gauge. All ties shall be carefully adzed before plates are applied.

493 Broken rail in track will be reported at once to the Supervisor of Track on the proper blanks. Broken rails.

494 When new rail is being laid and surfaced it must be perfectly lined according to stakes set by the Supervisor of Track, as no imperfection in alignment will be permitted. Joint and intermediate ties shall be respaced to conform with standard plan. Lining and laying new rails.

495 On tangents and curves of six degrees and under the track should be laid and maintained to exact standard gauge, 4 feet 8½ inches. On curves over six degrees widen gauge by use of iron shims according to the following table: Gauge.

6 degrees to 10 degrees, ¼ inch.
10 degrees to 14 degrees, ½ inch.
14 degrees to 18 degrees, ¾ inch.
18 degrees and over, 1 inch.

496 During October and November of each year track gauges shall be sent to the Supervisor of Track for comparison with the division standard gauge, and all gauges so tested will be painted a new color each year to indicate that they have been inspected. Inspection gauges.

497 Use particular care to gauge correctly at joints, especially where the anglebar projection is liable to catch the lug of the gauge. Gauging at joints.

498 During the winter months test the gauge of all tracks, and respike the rails where necessary to obtain correct gauge. Winter gauging.

499 On all tangents the track must be perfectly level tranversely, except as provided in Rule 503, and Level board.

great care must be exercised by foremen in the use and adjustment of track level. During the month of December each year track levels shall be sent to the Supervisor of Track for adjustment and painting of the same color as tested track gauges.

Elevation on curves.

500 Consult the Supervisor of Track regarding each curve on your section, and obtain from him the proper elevation, according to the speed of trains.

Method of ascertaining degree of curves.

501 To determine the degree of a curve stretch a sixty-two foot line with a small knot at the center (which will be 31 feet from either end) on the running side of a well-lined portion of a curve. Measure the distance from the knot to the running side of the rail, and every inch of this distance indicates one degree of curvature.

Re-lining curves.

502 To re-line curves in the absence of centre-stakes stretch the string straight on the running side of the rail with one end at the beginning of the curve, and measure the distance from the knot to the running side of rail. Repeat this operation for the entire length of the curve, and divide the sum of these measurements by the total number taken. The result will be the average measurement which should be used in re-lining the curve.

Elevating curves.

503 "Simple" curves should have full elevation at the point of curve, and the same elevation should be used uniformly for the entire length of the curve. For elevations of 3 inches and under the rate of the run-off on the tangents should be $\frac{1}{4}$ inch per rail length of 30 feet. For elevations over 3 inches the run-off should not exceed 12 rail lengths or 360 feet.

Compound curves should have the elevation increased or decreased on each section of the curve corresponding to the change in degree. The change in elevation should be distributed one-half on each section.

The run-off on transition or easement curves should be made on the easement.

As a practical rule, the following rates of elevation will meet usual conditions:

503-a Main Passenger Tracks: Curves under 2 degrees the elevation should be twice the middle ordinate of a 62 foot string. Curves 2 degrees and over add 2 inches to the middle ordinate of a 62 foot string.

503-b Main Freight Tracks: Three-fourths the middle ordinate of a 62 foot string.

503-c Combination Tracks: Middle ordinate of a 62 foot string.

503-d Side Tracks: No elevation.

Maximum elevation 8 inches.

This rule should be modified to meet special conditions.

Table for elevating curves.

504 The following table will be a guide to the study of special conditions, and gives the amounts of elevation for each degree of curvature for various speeds:

Degrees of Curve.	Speed in miles per hour.				
	20	30	40	50	60
1	¼ in.	½ in.	1 in.	1¾ in.	2½ in.
2	½ "	1¼ "	2¼ "	3½ "	5 "
3	¾ "	1¾ "	3¼ "	5 "	7¼ "
4	1 "	2½ "	4½ "	6¾ "	——
5	1¼ "	3 "	5½ "	——	
6	1¾ "	3¾ "	6½		
7	2 "	4¼ "	7½		
8	2¼ "	5 "	8¾		
9	2½ "	5½ "	——		
10	2¾ "	6¼ "			
11	3 "	6¾ "			
12	3¼ "	7¼ "			
13	3½ "	8			
14	3¾ "	——			
15	4¼ "				
16	4½ "				

Switches and frogs.

505 All switches and frogs must be laid in accordance with standard plans; they must be kept well lined and in good surface. Care shall be taken in laying new switches to see that the switch point is placed at the heights shown on the standard plan so as to prevent the back of wheels from turning over the stock rail.

Daily inspection switches and frogs.

506 Foremen and track walkers must give careful daily attention to switches and see that they work easily and with no lost motion; that all bolts and nuts are tight and that they are otherwise in safe condition. When cotter or keeper pins are not used in connection with rod bolts, the bolts must be nicked with a chisel to prevent turning of nuts.

Snow and ice.

507 During cold weather ice and snow must be removed from frogs and switches, station platforms, flangeways at crossings, and track scales. Ice must be removed from the roof, sides and bottoms of tunnels. Undue quantities of snow and ice, including icicles on roofs of buildings, must be removed.

Track walking.

508 Pass over your section at least once every other day, and see that it is walked and examined every morning by the track-walker, to see that everything affecting traffic is safe. See that all gates to private crossings are kept closed when not in use, that cars standing on sidings properly clear the main track, and that derailing switches are properly set. The track-walker must report at once any defects he cannot repair.

Bridge warnings.

509 Section foremen are responsible for the proper maintenance of bridge warnings, and will promptly replace any portion of the " ticklers " that may be missing or misplaced. See that the proper height is maintained from the top of rail to the bottom of ticklers.

Policing.

510 Policing is most essential in order to give the roadbed and surroundings a neat and clean appearance. Station surroundings must be kept clean and in good order. Telegraph lines, owned by the company, mileposts, whistle-boards, bridge-boards and other standard signs, must be kept in good order, and trees near wires owned by the company should be kept trimmed to prevent the branches from touching the lines during storms or high winds.

Old material. **511** All old material, such as old ties, rails, splices, material dropped from cars, etc., must be picked up and carefully piled at proper points; no litter nor refuse of any kind will be permitted on the right of way of the company. Station grounds and all places frequented by employes or the public must be kept free from obstructions over which persons may trip or fall.

512 All refuse and dirt in the Park Avenue tunnel must be placed in neat piles; under street bridges between tracks 2 and 3.

513 Dirt material or snow must not be placed so as to obstruct the view of signals.

Right of way. **514** Acquaint yourselves with the boundary lines of the company's right of way, and under no circumstances allow any encroachment thereon by outside parties, except by permission of proper officers.

Grass, brush and weeds. **515** Weeds, trees and underbrush, grass, etc., must be kept close to the ground, and cleared away from bridges and trestles, mile and sign-posts, and other perishable material and structures, so that the dry vegetation will not allow fire to communicate to them.

Time to cut grass. **516** Clear right or way from grass, weeds and brush between 15th and 25th days of June and between the 15th and 25th days of August each year.

Watchmen. **517** See that watchmen are properly detailed to watch bridges, to patrol unsafe or imperfect track, or to perform other duties guarding the safety of the track and structures, and frequently visit these men at such intervals, day or night, to determine whether their duties are being faithfully performed. Any watchman unfaithful to his duty shall be immediately discharged by the foreman.

518 Promptly report in writing to the Supervisor of Track any failure of trainmen to respect your signal, giving the number of train and engine. Observing signals.

519 In case of accident to a train, the nearest section foreman will take his entire force to the assistance of the train. If notified of a broken rail he will at once make the necessary repairs. Accidents.

520 When assisting a train delayed by accident, act under the directions of the conductor until the arrival of the Supervisor of Track or wrecking foreman. Directions during accidents.

521 In cases of wreck, you must at once appoint watchmen to look after the company's property, who will remain on duty until the goods are removed. Watchmen at wrecks.

522 In case of accident to trains or roadbed, or injury of any kind, **no matter how trivial,** to anyone in their employ, foremen must immediately make a report by wire to the Supervisor of Track, and shall follow up this report as soon possible with a written report. Reports.

523 If from any cause there is an accident, or the track becomes obstructed, and the section foreman cannot promptly repair the damage, the Supervisor of Track and Superintendent or Train Master must be advised by wire immediately. Telegraph reports.

524 All highway and farm crossings must be kept in the best possible repair, free from all obstructions to Highways and farm crossings.

vision or travel. Hand or push-cars must not be left unnecessarily on crossings. Farm-crossing gates must be promptly repaired when out of order, and must be kept closed when not in actual use.

Crossing planks.

525 All crossings must be kept in accordance with standard plan. Defective or loose crossing plank must be promptly fastened or renewed. Care must be taken to see that crossing planks are not heaved up so as to project above the top of the rails.

Sidings.

526 All company sidings must be maintained in as good order as practicable, **especially adjacent to main tracks.** The owners of private sidings must be required to keep their sidings in a safe condition for use at all times. If they fail to do so the switch must be spiked and the Supervisor promptly notified.

Side obstructions.

527 Be careful that wood, cross-ties, lumber or other material is not piled closer than eight feet from the rail of the main track, and five feet from the rail of sidings. Signal or telegraph poles must not be placed nearer to the rail than eight feet, and telegraph poles, where possible, will be placed near the right of way line. Also notice that cars on sidings give the proper clearance. Frequently examine foundations of buildings, etc., lumber or log piles or similar structures which are close to the tracks, whether the same are owned by this company or by private parties, and whether the same are located on this company's property or on private land, and report to the Supervisor of Track any that show signs of weakness, so that proper steps may be taken to make repairs before the tracks are obstructed.

528 During extremely cold weather, when water-stations are likely to freeze, foremen, if called upon by the Supervisor of Track, will send a man to the station, who will keep it in such condition that engines can take water at all times. Water-stations.

529 Jacks must never be placed on the inside of the rail. When raised they should immediately be placed in tripping position. They must always be in the hands of experienced men. Jacks.

530 Hand and push-cars must not be allowed to stand on the track, and care must be taken to have them clear of passing trains. Hand and push-cars.

531 When the car is not in sight of the foreman it must be kept locked. Loaded push or hand-cars must not be run on the main track, except under the protection of a red flag as specified in paragraph 65. Protection of cars.

532 Hand or push-cars must never be attached to moving trains. Rails must not be carried on hand-cars, except in cases of emergency. Great care must be exercised in using hand-cars during foggy weather or after dark. Cars must not be run at night or on Sunday, except in cases of actual necessity, and never for personal use. Cars carrying men must not be coupled together, and must be run not less than 2000 feet apart. Use of cars.

533 Foremen must always accompany velocipedes or hand or push-cars. Foremen accompany cars.

Permits. **534** Only employes of the Railroad Company in the discharge of their duties will be permitted on the tracks of the company, on velocipedes, motor-cars, hand-cars or push-cars, unless special permits in writing are given by the Engineer Maintenance of Way or the Manager, after the necessary release has been signed.

Trespass. **535** Bicyclists and other trespassers shall not be permitted on the right-of-way of the company.

Unsafe cars. **536** Cars in unsafe condition must not be used, but the Supervisor of Track should be immediately notified of the fact.

Use of material. **537** Proper judgment and caution must be exercised against extravagant use of material, as you will be held strictly responsible for the same.

Account for material. **538** Will be held strictly responsible for all materials, tools, etc., in your possession, and, when called upon to do so, must be able to account for everything in your charge.

Protection of material. **539** All material and tools must be kept locked in section-houses wherever possible.

Old spikes. **540** When spikes are drawn from the tracks they must be carefully removed, with a view to using them again. Old ties must never be thrown away with spikes left in them.

Repairs to tools. **541** Tools, hand-cars, etc., requiring repairs that cannot be made by the foreman, must be properly tagged and sent to the company's repair shop. Each article so shipped must be plainly marked with the name and address of the foreman to whom it is to be returned.

542 Each foreman may employ his own men, and may suspend or discharge them for incompetency or insubordination. Employing men.

543 The time book must be written up every night for the day just closed, the time of the foremen and men being kept for each kind of work performed, under the proper heading. Time books, together with the material reports of all tools and materials received and used during the month, must be forwarded by the foreman to the Supervisor of Track on the days directed. Time books.

544 Properly fill out all blanks as directed by the Supervisor of Track. Blanks.

545 All signal piping, wires, and other signal apparatus must be kept free from ballast, track material, crossing plank, and other obstructions that will interfere with the free working of signals. **Where electric circuits are in use, all ballast, cinders, etc., must be kept from the base of rail.** Fibre insulators, and end posts on insulating joints, must be renewed when necessary. Signal obstructions.

Drawbridge Tenders.

546 Drawbridge tenders report to and receive instruction from the Supervisor, and will obey orders from the Superintendent concerning the movement of trains.

Examination. **547** Pass the examination required as to:

Character, habits, and records of previous service.

Knowledge of Time-table, rules and regulations.

Also, for color perception, strength of vision and hearing.

548 Be constantly at their posts, be provided with necessary signals and tools, and know that everything connected with the draw and signals is in working order.

Appliances. **549** Know the time when each regular train should pass the point where they are stationed, notice all signals displayed for sections of trains, and keep a vigilant watch for extras. Do not rely upon whistles or bells.

Signals disarranged. **550** Should the signals become disarranged, station flagmen with hand signals at the location of the defective fixed signals, and know that trains are protected before opening the draw.

Duty. **551** Display danger signals immediately if any switch is out of order, or there is any obstruction on the track endangering trains.

Opening of drawbridges. **552** The draw must not be opened until the proper signals have been shown a sufficient length of time, and far enough in each direction to ensure the stoppage of an approaching train. Extra precautions must be taken whenever flags or lights cannot be distinctly seen. Danger signals must not be changed to safety until the draw is closed and locked.

Statute laws. **553** Be familiar with the statute laws with relation to drawbridges on railroads, and observe the special rules relating to the drawbridge under your charge. Provide yourself with a copy of the current Time-table, and report any unusual delay to any train at your bridge, with an explanation of the cause. Keep a record of detentions to all vessels, showing name of vessel, date, length of delay, and cause.

554 Drawbridge Bell Code.

2 bells, unlock draw.

3 bells, closing draw.

1 bell, draw is closed ready to lock.

5 bells, unlock draw quickly.

Above to be answered from tower by two bells.

Bell code to be used from 126th Street tower to drawbridge for flagging trains by signal.

Track No. 3 — 3 — 1. Signal No. 11 has failed. Section is clear, flag train by signal.

Track No. 4 — 4. Signal No. 5 has failed. Section is clear, flag train by signal.

Answer by bridgeman to towerman by 2 bells.

Work-Train Conductors.

555 Conductors of work-trains will be under the immediate direction of the Supervisor of Track; must obey the orders of the Superintendent regarding the movement of their trains, shall faithfully observe all train rules and shall familiarize themselves with all kinds of work pertaining to the maintenance of track. General duties.

Reports. **556** Make all reports as directed, and at the close of each day send to the Supervisor of Track a written report of all delays to their trains during the day, owing to not having received orders promptly, or from any other cause, and also report the work accomplished during the day.

Delays. **557** When a work-train is delayed take immediate steps to employ the time of the men. In such cases the force can be employed to good advantage in cleaning station grounds, ditching, ballasting, etc.

Accidents. **558** In case of train accident, work-trains will give such assistance as may be called for by the Superintendent, and everything shall be done to facilitate the quick and safe movement of trains.

Daily programme. **559** The duties of the work-train shall be arranged in advance, so as to require the least amount of lost time passing over the road.

Supervisor of Signals.

General duties. **560** The Supervisor of Signals reports to the Engineer Maintenance of Way, and is responsible for the proper installation, maintenance and safe condition of all block signals, interlocking plants, train order signals, drawbridge signals, distant switch and station signals, and such other appliances as may be assigned to him. Will have charge of Inspectors, Foremen—Pneumatic, Mechanical and Electrical Repairmen—Batterymen, Helpers, Lampmen, Flagmen, Linemen, Carpenters, Painters, and others employed on signal work.

561 Personally instruct subordinates in proper methods of construction and maintenance with a view to efficiency and economy. Instruction of men.

562 Give each man specific instructions as to the limits of the work to which he is assigned. Fixed limits of responsibility.

563 Prepare plans and estimates for signaling, and submit them to the Engineer Maintenance of Way. Plans and estimates.

564 Do not make any change in the location of signals or in the locking, or in the methods of operation without the written authority of the Engineer Maintenance of Way, who must first secure the approval of the Manager. Changes.

565 Make such examinations of all appliances under your charge as to insure proper maintenance and adherence to standards. Inspection.

566 Inspect and make detail daily reports on the condition of signal appliances on the district, or on any construction work to which you may be assigned.

567 Make frequent inspections to see that all signals are kept bright and in proper adjustment and focus, and the lights kept in good order. Proper display of signals.

568 During each quarter make a personal examination of all signal appliances under your charge, and on the last day of March, June, September and December render duplicate reports in detail on standard inspection blanks, to the Engineer Maintenance of Way. Quarterly inspections.

569 Use special care in placing and sighting signals to see that they present a good view and have a good background. Locating signals.

Plumb signal masts and pole line. **570** See that all signal masts and pole lines are kept plumb and that wire lines are neatly run.

Neat surroundings. **571** See that the surroundings of all towers are kept neat and clean, and promptly report to the Engineer Maintenance of Way any cases where work should be done by men in other branches of the service in order to keep the property neat in the neighborhood of signal apparatus.

Material neatly kept. **572** See that new material delivered out on the line is neatly piled, and the small parts are properly secured from theft; also see that all old material is promptly removed from view of main tracks. No litter or refuse of any kind will be permitted on the right of way.

Responsibility for keys. **573** Keep a book record of all keys for signal appliances issued, take a receipt for them and see that they are issued only to those whose duties require their use.

Storms. **574** In case of storm see that enough men are kept on interlockings to prevent detentions to trains.

Following up failures. **575** In case of failure of any signal apparatus, personally investigate the trouble, see that it is promptly corrected, and immediately make report to the Engineer Maintenance of Way, giving the nature and cause of the trouble and the action taken to prevent repetition.

Restoring apparatus in service. **576** When any signal apparatus has been cut out of service personally follow up the case to see that regular working is promptly restored.

577 Where the assistance of track forces are required application shall be made to the Supervisor of Track. Assistance of track forces.

578 Keep a complete file of plans for each interlocking plant and block signal installation, or other signal device as follows: File of plans

Plan A. General arrangement of Signals giving distances, including the "clear view" of each distant, home and advance signal.

Plan B. Detail layout of pipe and wire runs showing signals, cranks, wheels, compensators, foundations, track circuits, underground wires, line wires and cables, batteries, track relays, and any other data necessary for an intelligent understanding of the design of the plant. Manipulation sheet.

Plan C. Locking sheet, dog diagram with skeleton diagram of track.

Plan D. Signal plan issued for Operating Department in installing plant.

Plan E. Each signal tower shall be supplied with a manipulation sheet.

579 Keep the characteristic sheets of signal work up to date. Characteristic sheets.

580 Keep detail records and prepare statements showing cost of installation and maintenance of all work under your charge. Record of cost of installation and maintenance.

581 On maintenance inspection visit all towers and signal appliances both day and night at irregular intervals, and inspect every detail of the apparatus, including the condition of the tower. Maintenance inspection.

Conduct of signalmen. **582** Note the conduct of the signalmen with a view to determining their capacity for properly handling the signal appliances.

Check up material, and sample. **583** Check up and inspect all material received, before it is put into the work.

Nature of reports. **584** Keep daily account of the men employed and their rates of pay, the amount of material used, and render force and material reports on standard blank forms.

Signal Foremen.

General duties. **585** All foremen report to and receive their instructions from the Supervisor of Signals. May be assigned to either construction work or to a district of maintenance work and are responsible for the proper installation and maintenance of all work under their charge in accordance with standard rules, plans and specifications.

Limits of work defined. **586** Will receive specific instructions as to the limits of the work under their charge, but will always be subject to special call for duty on other sections in cases of emergency.

Personnel of gangs. **587** Will be responsible for the selection of competent and intelligent men for their gangs, and instruct them in the proper execution of their work.

Reports. **588** Make daily reports in detail, giving the nature of the work done, and render reports of labor and material on standard forms.

Time. **589** Make out time books for the men under their charge, and be responsible for their correctness.

Repairmen

590 All signal repairmen report to and receive their instructions from the Supervisor of Signals. Are responsible for the inspection, adjustment and proper maintenance of all interlockings, block signals and other appliances assigned to their care, and the proper execution of any construction work of which they may be put in charge. General duties.

591 Do not make any alterations or additions to the work under their charge without written instructions from the Supervisor of Signals. Make no change without instruction.

592 When it is necessary to do any work requiring the disarrangement of locking devices, the repairman in charge shall first obtain written authority from the Supervisor of Signals, including instructions as to the time that the work shall be done. Before starting the work wire the Superintendent and obtain his O. K. for authority. Then personally notify the towerman and note on the train sheet of the tower the words "Locking disarranged," giving the numbers of the levers affected, the time at which the work is started and his signature. Before disarranging the locking first disconnect all switches and signals affected by the work, and spike the switches in their normal position, thus insuring the proper protection of all movements involved in the disarrangement of the locking. When the work is complete and the locking restored, personally notify the towerman and note on train sheet the words "Locking restored," giving the time at which the work is completed and his signature. Then wire Procedure in working on interlocking.

the Superintendent and the Supervisor of Signals that the work is complete.

During the time that the locking is disarranged trains shall be forwarded by clearance cards same as for any failure of the apparatus.

Procedure in disconnecting movements.

593 No movement shall be disconnected or circuit cut out except in case of actual necessity, but when such necessity exists the repairman shall first notify the towerman and note on the train sheet the words "———— No.——— disconnected," inserting the name of the movement in the first blank space and the number of the lever in the second, together with the time and his signature. When the movement is again connected up and regular working restored, he shall note under his previous note the words " Regular working restored," again giving the time and his signature.

Protection with movements disconnected.

594 If necessary to disconnect any switch, facing point lock, detector bar or drawbridge lock, electric circuit, or any similar device affecting the safety of the track, first confer with the section foreman and arrange for the proper protection of the track by flagmen under the section foreman's direction.

Fasten at danger all signals protecting the movements to be disconnected, and personally see that the flagmen are properly protecting the tracks concerned before any movement is disconnected. Whenever a switch or movable point frog is disconnected it must be spiked in position before any train is permitted to pass over it.

595 Adjust switches and movable point frogs with a standard switch gauge, and if the gauge of the track is incorrect or the stock rail is improperly bent ahead of the points so that they do not face up properly, notify the section foreman in writing, and if the necessary change is not promptly made notify the Supervisor of Signals. In the meantime the points must be adjusted to fit the stock rails as they are, so that there may be no possible chance of a wheel taking the wrong side of a point. If by any chance the gauge should be so defective as to render such adjustment impossible, the repairman shall disconnect the switch and spike it in the normal position, also disconnecting the signal for any diverting movement over that switch. Make record of the occurrence on the train sheet in accordance with Rule No. 592 and notify the Superintendent and the Supervisor of Signals by wire and follow up the case and see that regular working is restored as promptly as possible. Adjusting switch and frog movements.

596 In connecting new work, switch points must be kept spiked until the signals governing movements over them are connected up. Connecting up new switches.

597 In the case of automatic signals where there is no towerman or train sheet, be careful to fasten signals at danger before doing any work or interfering with the apparatus in any way that might render it possible for a signal to give a false indication. Securing automatic signals at danger.

598 No apparatus shall be cut out of service without the authority of the Supervisor of Signals, and then only after notice by wire has been sent by the repairman to the Superintendent for his information. Nothing to be cut out without instructions.

Report improper condition of track work.

599 Whenever the condition of switches or track work does not admit of proper operation or maintenance of the signal work, the fact must be reported to the Supervisor of Signals and the Supervisor of Track in writing.

Apparatus kept locked.

600 See that all block instruments, electric locks, relay boxes, battery wells, automatic signals, crossing bell boxes, and other devices requiring protection are equipped with locks and that they are kept locked.

Procedure in working on block instruments.

601 If necessary to take a case off of a block instrument or electric lock confer with the towerman, and if possible select a time when there is no train in the block ahead, or any probability of one approaching from the rear. In all cases first note on the train sheet of the tower, the number of the track on which you are going to work, the position of the card and the time, with your signature. While the case is off, the block instrument must not be used. Trains must be forwarded by clearance card in same manner as for any failure ot the apparatus. When the work is complete and the case replaced on the instrument and locked, note on the train sheet the words "Regular working restored, track No. ——," together with the time and your signature.

Not leave tower while case is off.

602 Do not leave the tower while the case is off the block instrument or electric lock, and in replacing the case be careful to see that the card is in the proper position.

Wrecks.

603 In case of wreck in which signal apparatus may be in any way concerned, go on the ground as promptly as possible, and note the situation and the

condition of the signal apparatus. Immediately wire the Supervisor of Signals brief particulars of the occurrence.

In case the accident may have been caused or is alleged to have been caused by any defect in the signal apparatus, immediately make a thorough examination of everything in connection with the case and send a written statement of the condition you find to the Supervisor of Signals.

604 Repairmen are always subject to call unless they have special permission from the Supervisor of Signals to be relieved. Subject to call.

605 Always keep your headquarters telegraph office advised as to where you can be found, and respond promptly when called. Keep telegraph office advised.

606 If relieved from duty post in your headquarters telegraph office the name and telegraph call of the relief man. Relief notice.

607 Render all reports in accordance with schedules furnished by the Supervisor of Signals, and where your subordinates are required to make reports certify to their correctness and forward them to the Supervisor of Signals with your own. Reports.

608 In case of call to cover a failure, fill out the failure report form, giving the time at which notice of failure was received, the trains used in reaching the trouble, the cause of the trouble, the time trouble is corrected, and the time the report is forwarded to the Supervisor of Signals. Failure report.

Records of failures and detentions.

609 Records will be kept by the Supervisor of Signals showing the failures charged to each repairman and the train detentions due to each failure, and these records will assist in determining the relative efficiency of the men.

Renewals to be made before failure may occur.

610 Make frequent detail inspection of all the apparatus under your charge, and make renewals before any parts can deteriorate so that a failure may occur.

Movements to be kept tight and secure.

611 Take up lost motion and see that no studs, pins or holes are allowed to become worn more than 1-32 of an inch in any direction.

Cotter pins.

612 See that cotter pins are in place, in good condition and properly spread.

Foundations to be kept rigid and in line.

613 Keep all foundations rigid and level and in perfect line, and see that the distances from rail and elevations are kept in accordance with standard plans.

Signal masts plumb.

614 Keep all signal masts plumb.

Signal blades.

615 See that signal blades are kept bright, and notify the Supervisor of Signals if they need attention.

Bearings oiled and free from grit.

616 Keep the bearings of all moving parts free from grit. Care must be taken to use just the right amount of oil and not flood the parts oiled. Old oil must be removed and the parts wiped before re-oiling.

Adjustment of switches and facing point locks.

617 Inspect switches in operation each time you visit a tower, and see that the holes in the locking bars are not worn more than 1-16 of an inch in any direction. Plungers on facing point locks shall clear the locking bar one inch when withdrawn, and have a throw of eight inches. The ends must be kept square and not tapered or beveled. All switch points shall be so adjusted that they cannot be locked when a No. 9 signal wire is placed between the switch point and the stock rail.

618 Give lampmen necessary instructions and see that they perform their work properly. Instruct lampmen.

619 Pay particular attention to the fastenings of ladders to signal masts or bridges. Ladder fastenings.

620 If you find a broken or cracked glass in a signal lamp or semaphore casting renew it immediately, or if the necessary glass is not at hand, take off the lamp bracket and display a red light on the signal mast until the glass is renewed. Broken or cracked glass.

621 See that the dogs on interlocking are kept perfectly tight, and that the interlocking and latch blocks and quadrants are not allowed to become worn. Keep interlocking and latches tight.

622 See that there is proper drainage to carry water away from pipes, wires and movements at signal towers, that section foremen keep ballast cinders, etc., free from base of rail where electric circuit is in use, and that fibre insulations and fibre end posts are renewed in Weber joints and insulated switch rods by the section foreman when required. If these points do not receive proper attention promptly notify the Supervisor of Signals. Drainage, etc.

623 See that wheels run freely and that there is no chance for wires to jam. Wheels free

624 See that chains are sufficiently long to prevent the split links or wire eyes reaching the wheel No split links over wheels when the signal is thrown. A split link must not be used to splice a chain where it passes over a wheel. The ends of split links must be closed.

No attachments on masts.

625 Do not permit any foreign wires or any attachment foreign to the apparatus to be placed on signal masts.

Adjusting screws.

626 See that all signals are provided with the proper number of adjusting screws, that they are kept in good condition and the thread free from paint or rust.

Tag wires.

627 See that all wires running to relays or lightning arresters are tagged to show their functions.

Clean contacts.

628 Keep contacts carefully cleaned and in perfect adjustment.

Tests for defects.

629 Frequently test for defects, and where any indication of defect is found remove the defective part and forward it to the Supervisor of Signals with an explanation of the trouble.

Ordering material.

630 Send monthly requisitions to the Supervisor of Signals for tools or materials that you require for yourselves and your assistants, but in case of actual emergency you may call on the storekeeper direct by wire or letter for material required. The storekeeper will furnish it, but will send such requests to the Supervisor of Signals, so that they may be inspected and the reason for the emergency order ascertained.

Improvements.

631 Repairmen are expected to make any recommendations for improvements that they may consider desirable.

632 The following rules pertain to the use of torpedo machines as audible signals in addition to the fixed signal: Torpedo machines

632-a Where torpedo machines are in use the gauge of track shall be exact standard gauge and shall not be widened for any reason.

632-b Torpedo machines must always be used in duplicate—one for each rail.

632-c There shall be a space of one-sixteenth of an inch between the head of the rail and top of torpedo exploder or anvil.

632-d The top of torpedo exploder or anvil shall stand level with the top of rail when unloaded.

632-e The torpedo exploder or anvil when raised by the lifter arms must clear the under side of housing to prevent the torpedoes jamming against the bottom edge of the exploder.

632-f The torpedo slide must be moved its full stroke in order to properly receive the torpedo from the magazine. A cam or idle movement to be used so as to insure full stroke regardless of variation in the connections between machine and lever.

632-g The machines must be inspected daily and kept cleaned and properly oiled.

632-h The bottom torpedo must never be allowed to remain in service long enough to wear away the metal of the torpedo shell.

632-i Whenever necessary to throw a torpedo machine out of service a man must be continually stationed at the machine to clamp track torpedoes on the rail whenever the signal is in a danger position.

632-j Torpedoes must be carefully handled. They are likely to explode if roughly treated.

632-k They must be kept in dry places. They must not be left in contact with brick walls, damp wood, chloride of lime or other disinfectant; they must not be exposed to the action of steam or other vapor.

632-l The date on which torpedoes are received must be marked on the boxes in which they are shipped. They must be considered defective after they are two years old or when they bear any signs of rust on the outside of the case. Any such defective torpedoes must be withdrawn from stock and returned to the storehouse.

632-m Torpedoes must be issued for service and used in the order in which they are received. Those which have been on hand the longest always being used first, to avoid any accumulation of old stock.

632-n Should any torpedo fail to explode when a train passes over it, the circumstance must be promptly reported to the Supervisor of Signals and the defective torpedo properly marked and forwarded to him for examination.

632-o All torpedo machines must be tested at least once a week by exploding a torpedo in each machine.

Batterymen.

633 Batterymen report to and receive their instructions from the repairmen. They are responsible for the proper condition of all batteries and connections under their charge, and for the proper care and use of the material furnished to them. General duties.

634 Keep all battery wells and lockers clean — and locked — no refuse material shall be left around the batteries. Battery wells.

635 See that batteries are kept at an even temperature, protected from extreme heat or cold, and that the jars are kept clean and bright and free from salts. Care of batteries.

636 Collect all scrap zincs and copper taken from batteries, at headquarters, and send it to the storekeeper the first of each month. Nothing that has any value should be thrown away. Scrap.

637 Batterymen shall act as relief men for repairmen as they may be assigned, and shall post themselves fully on the repairmen's work. Act as relief.

638 Do not make any changes in wiring or connections without instructions in writing from the repairman. No changes without instructions

639 Jumpers will be provided for cutting out cells and care must be used never to open a normally closed circuit in removing cells. Jumpers.

640 In renewing track battery, never have more than one cell out of service at one time. Track battery.

Emptying batteries.

641 Do not empty any battery solution or throw any refuse on the roadbed or bridges or in small streams.

Maintenance of gravity batteries.

642 The following rule will be observed in the maintenance of gravity batteries:

642-a All gravity zincs must be cleaned ten days after the cell has been set up, and every three weeks thereafter.

642-b A zinc that is more than half consumed must not be used in track battery. When it is half consumed it must be transferred to one of the main battery cells.

642-c The zincs in all main block batteries are to be used, wherever practicable, until consumed to one-quarter their original weight.

642-d All battery connections must be inspected at each visit, and no elements with poor or unsafe connections shall be left in the circuit.

642-e If stalactites form on the zincs they must not be scraped off and allowed to drop in the cell. The zincs must be removed and cleaned.

642-f Gravity batteries give the best results with the bottom of the zinc at a distance of two and one-half inches above the top of copper. Adjustable zincs shall be kept as nearly as possible at that distance. The bottom of the zinc should never be less than two inches or more than three and one-half inches from the top of the copper.

642-g Before placing copper element in cell examine it carefully and see that the parts are properly riveted together and that the copper connecting wire is properly attached to one of the leaves.

642-h Copper connecting wires with defective or improper insulation must not be used.

642-i Copper elements that have not a full number of leaves or that present less than two-thirds of the original surface must not be left in the circuit.

642-j In order to prevent creeping of salts, copper connecting wires must stand away from side of the jar and must not be bent over the edge.

642-k In renewing cells all blue vitriol that remains in the cell must be carefully cleaned and used.

642-l All cells are to be charged with three pounds of blue vitriol crystals — dust must not be used.

642-m In renewing a cell save about one pint of the old zinc sulphate solution, and after the elements and the blue vitriol and water have been placed in the jar, pour the old solution gently on top of the zinc and add a sufficient amount of water to bring the top of the solution to within one inch of the top of the jar.

642-n After it becomes necessary to move a cell or add water, great care must be taken not to disturb the line of demarcation between the two solutions.

642-o After a cell has been set up, blue vitriol must not be added until the cell is again renewed.

642-p The object is to get as long life as possible from the battery, but to avoid any possibility of its becoming too weak to do the work required.

642-q If a jar cracks at all, it must be promptly cut out and removed from the circuit.

642-r Zinc sulphate solution must never register less than 15 degrees or more than 30 degrees. If the density of the zinc solution becomes too great a portion must be drawn out and clear water added.

642-s In renewing cells the loose copper in the jars must be carefully saved and together with scrap zinc or any defective new zinc must be taken to headquarters.

642-t Blue vitriol deteriorates very rapidly when exposed to heat or the action of the atmosphere.

Lampmen and Tunnel Flagmen

General duties. **643** Report to and receive their instructions from the Interlocking foreman, and are responsible for the condition of all lights under their charge and for the proper maintenance of any interlockings that may be assigned to them.

Examination. **644** Pass the examination required as to:

Character, habits and record of previous service.

Knowledge of Time-table, rules and regulations.

Also, for color perception, strength of vision, and hearing.

645 Protect the rear of any train stopped in the section—this regardless of the action of the flagman of train or position of block signals. Duty.

646 Be on duty during the prescribed hours, taking such precautions as will insure safety of trains. See that signals are all in working order, reporting promptly any defect which cannot be repaired at once.

647 Be provided with proper signals, and if track is obstructed, or from any cause the safety of trains is endangered, the red signals must be promptly and distinctly displayed, and no effort spared to warn approaching trains in time. This must always be done without reference to block signals. In case it is foggy, stormy, or in the night, or tunnel is filled with smoke, use torpedoes in addition to regular danger signal. Extra precautions.

648 Inspect all switches, signals, torpedo machines and connections under your charge at least twice a day, and keep them in good working order. If any defect is discovered, make prompt report to the repairman, and see that traffic is properly protected until the trouble is corrected. Use special care to make necessary changes in adjustment of signals during rapid changes in temperature. Inspect and keep in working order.

649 They are subject to call at all times and shall live where they can be called quickly in case of emer gency. Subject to call.

650 Keep the tower, windows, and the machinery neat and clean. Clean tower.

651 Take care of tower stove and remove ashes. Care of fire.

Fire protection. **652** See that fire buckets are kept filled and that fire extinguishers are in place and in good order.

Oily waste. **653** See that no oily waste is kept around the tower where a fire might occur from spontaneous combustion.

See that closet is kept clean. **654** Notify the foreman if the water closet requires cleaning or repairing.

Keep vicinity of tower neat. **655** Keep the entire property in the immediate vicinity of towers neat and free from rubbish.

Act as repairmen. **656** When so directed act as repairmen for the towers to which you are assigned.

Snow and ice. **657** Co-operate with the section men in keeping the movements clear of snow and ice.

Keep switch points clear. **658** See that switch points are kept free of obstructions.

Account of material. **659** Keep a careful account of all oil, wicks, burners, waste and other supplies used at the towers under your care, and furnish reports to the foreman.

Avoid showing light along track. **660** When putting signal lamps in place on the masts, be careful not to allow the light to show along the track so that it could in any way be mistaken for a clear signal. After placing lamps inspect them from the ground to see that they show the proper light.

Lamp failures. **661** Report all lamp failures, with the cause, on forms provided for that purpose.

Worn parts. **662** Return worn out burners or other worn out parts to the storekeeper.

663 Place all lamps on masts by sunset, and do not remove them until after sunrise. In dark or stormy weather they must be continued in service. Time for putting up lamps.

664 In the tunnel lamps must be kept burning day and night.

665 Comply with the following instructions for the care of lamps: Care of lamps.

665-a Lamps must be cleaned and filled each day.

665-b They must not be filled higher than one-half inch below top of font.

665-c The wick must reach the bottom of the font and must move freely.

665-d Where there is a lamp room, the lamps must be kept there when not in use, and must be lighted at least fifteen minutes before they are set out, and be burned low before the wick is turned up to full flame.

665-e When lamps are not lighted, the wicks must be kept below top of burner, to prevent oil overflowing.

665-f The fonts must be emptied once a week before refilling.

665-g The ventilating holes in burners must be kept open.

665-h The crust on wicks must be removed with the thumb and finger, or with a small stick. Wicks must not be cut unless they are irregular and have to be trimmed to secure a proper flame.

Burners and wicks.

666 Thoroughly clean the burners, especially air vent, and put in fresh wick at least once a month. See that the wick is neither too large nor too small to fit the burner, but turns up easily. See that all oil, soot, and dirt is wiped off the front and from inside of lanterns and lenses, and that all vents are kept open.

667 After lighting a lamp, do not turn up the wick beyond one-half full size of flame until the burner gets warm. If the flame flickers after lamp gets warm, look for the cause. See if the burner is bent; if so, straighten or replace. Report to proper authority any lamp which does not burn properly, so that it can be replaced and repaired.

668 Special tunnel flagmen who are engaged in a special duty through the Park Avenue tunnel will comply with the rules governing tunnel flagmen, with the exception that they must not leave their posts under any circumstances during their hours of duty until they have been relieved.

DIAGRAMS OF TRAIN SIGNALS.

Engine running forward as an extra train.

White lights and White flags at **A A.**

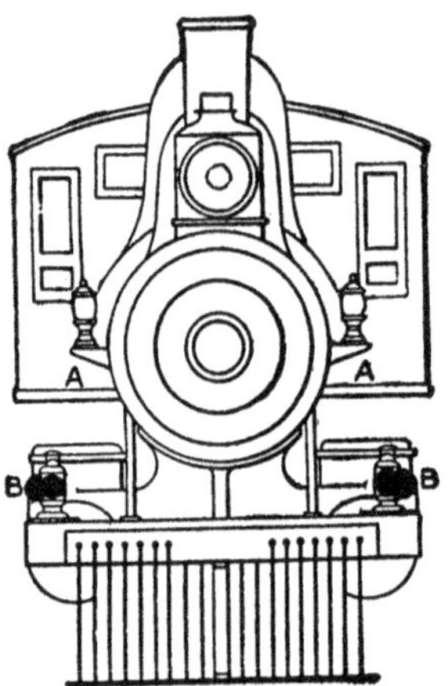

Engine running backward as an extra train, without cars.

Lights at **B B,** as markers, showing Green at side and in direction engine is moving, and Red in opposite direction.

Engine running forward displaying signals for a following section.

Green lights and Green flags at **A A.**

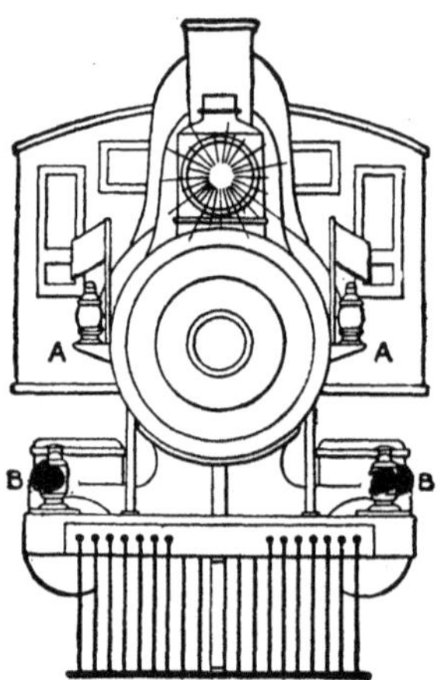

Engine running backward, at the rear of a train pushing cars.

Lights at **B B,** as markers, showing Green at side and in direction engine is moving, and Red in opposite direction.

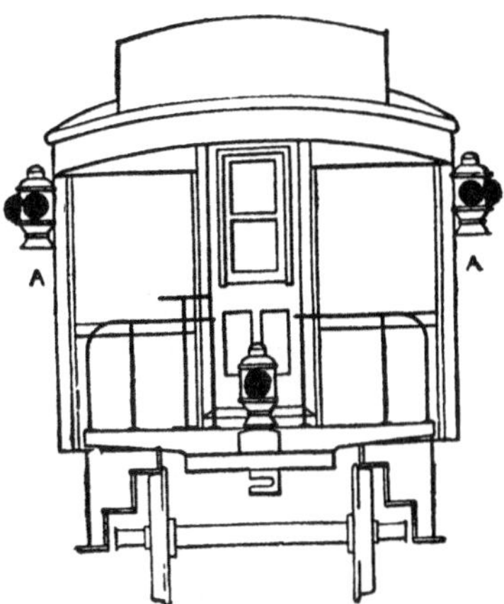

Rear of train while running.

Lights at **A A,** as markers, showing Green toward engine and side and Red to rear.

Engine running forward without cars or at the rear of a train pushing cars.

Lights at **A A,** as markers, showing Green to the front and side and Red to rear.

Engine running backward, without cars or at the front of a train pulling cars.
White light at **A.**

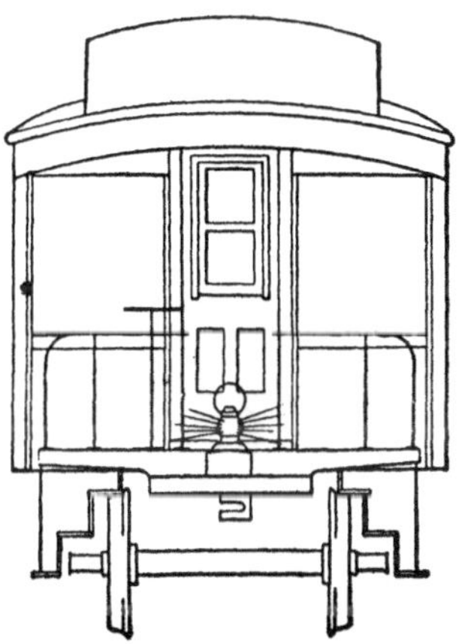

Passenger cars being pushed by an engine.
White light on front of leading car.

www.ingramcontent.com/pod-product-compliance
Lightning Source LLC
LaVergne TN
LVHW011232110826
845150LV00006B/1614

* 9 7 8 1 4 2 5 5 1 5 0 3 4 *